Dealing
with
Difficult
People

Dealing
with
Difficult
People

How to Deal with Nasty Customers,
Demanding Bosses and Annoying Co-workers

Roberta Cava

FIREFLY BOOKS

A FIREFLY BOOK

Published by Firefly Books (U.S.) Inc. 2004

First Printing

Publisher Cataloging-in-Publication Data (U.S.)

Cava, Roberta
        Dealing with difficult people : how to deal with nasty customers, demanding bosses and annoying co-workers / Roberta Cava. -- Rev. ed.
[232] p. : cm.
Includes index.
Summary: Strategies and useful techniques to help workers learn how to handle stressful situations. Includes effective communication skills, paraphrasing, feedback, interpreting body language and understanding different personality types.
ISBN 1-55297-927-X (pbk.)
1. 1. Interpersonal communication. 2. Work--Psychological aspects. 3. Interpersonal conflict. I. Title.
158.2'6   BF637.C45C37 2004

Published in the United States in 2004 by
Firefly Books (U.S.) Inc.
P.O. Box 1338, Ellicott Station
Buffalo, New York, USA
14205

Published in Canada in 2004 by Key Porter Books Limited.

Cover design: Peter Maher
Electronic formatting: Heidy Lawrance Associates

Printed and bound in Canada

CONTENTS

Dedicated to those seminar participants who have had to deal with difficult people and have passed on their ideas so others might benefit from their experience.

INTRODUCTION

Do you have to deal with irate, rude, impatient, emotional, persistent or aggressive people? Do you come home from work stressed out from having handled such people all day? If so, reading this book will enable you to control your moods by not allowing others to give you negative feelings. You'll learn how to control your anger and stress levels, and obtain a psychological edge by improving your people skills.

Businesses (especially those in the service sector) are learning the importance of having employees who are capable of handling all types of difficult people and situations. Employees who succeed in this area are in great demand.

Difficult people are the ones who try to:

- make us lose our cool;
- force us to do things we don't want to do;
- prevent us from doing what we want or need to do;
- often use coercion, manipulation or other underhanded methods to get their way;
- make us feel guilty if we don't go along with their wishes;
- make us anxious, upset, frustrated, angry, depressed, jealous, inferior, defeated or any other negative feeling;
- make us do their share of the work.

Knowing techniques *that work* for dealing with difficult people and situations can boost your confidence, improve your competence at work, reduce stress and anxiety, and increase your enthusiasm for your job.

You'll experience a feeling of accomplishment when you handle difficult situations well. Your employer, co-workers and staff will trust and rely on you, will admire and like you, will think twice before pushing you around and will be more willing to try to please you.

How do I know that the techniques outlined in this book really *work*? Because more than 45,000 participants worldwide have attended my seminar and have given their input. Many took the time to write to me with examples of how they dealt with particularly difficult situations. These contributions are scattered throughout the book. I endorse every technique described here and use them regularly. Not only do I handle difficult situations better, but I've gained control of my reactions to negative situations. So can you!

1

UNDERSTANDING BEHAVIOR AND ITS EFFECTS

Question: What is a difficult person? *Answer*: A person whose behavior causes difficulties—for you and others. Dealing with difficult people simply means dealing with difficult *behavior*. And recognizing that your actions or behavior can contribute to another person's difficult behavior.

This book is about the interaction between you and others. Interaction is a two-way street. You react to a person: the person reacts to you. We may not be able to control other people's behavior directly, but, by learning how to manage our own behavior and developing techniques for communicating effectively, we can influence other people in a positive way. We can turn their (and our own) difficult behavior into civilized, constructive behavior that allows all of us to think well of ourselves.

Learning to deal with difficult people involves learning how to manage *your* side of a two-way transaction. Doing so gives the other person a chance to work with you to resolve whatever is making him or her difficult.

When we encounter a difficult person, many of us react in ways that make the problem worse—for example, by responding with a sharp retort, by becoming defensive rather than attempting to deal with the real issue, by taking the person's anger personally. These natural but counterproductive responses reduce our chances of transforming a negative encounter into a constructive one.

For example, many times, when you are dealing with people who are irritable, rude, impatient or angry, you're not in a position to yell back. This is especially true if you work on the front lines for your company and run into difficult people either on the phone or in person. You can control your unproductive reaction if you mentally refuse to accept the negatives they're throwing at you.

Suppose that a client starts to bawl you out, really takes a strip off you, for something that wasn't your fault. What would your natural reaction be?

1. *You defend yourself or your company.*

Most of us respond this way. The client attacked you verbally, which triggered your defense mechanism. This response is instinctive, as natural for you as breathing. Does responding defensively usually solve anything? Not likely. Is this type of response going to satisfy the customer? Not likely. You could end up in a shouting match, creating negative feelings in both parties. This is a lose–lose situation.

2. *You're furious at the client's behavior but grit your teeth and concentrate on solving the problem.*

Even though you don't show it on the outside, inside you're seething. If you absorb the other person's anger, it will have to be removed later. Some people deal with this absorbed anger by barking at the next person they see, driving like a maniac on the way home from work, or going home and kicking the dog. Remember, you choose whether to accept another person's anger or not. If you do accept it, you've allowed the situation to get to you. This is a negative response—in this case, for you. Stop for a moment and ask yourself, "What is the client mad at—me or the situation?" In most cases, it's the situation. You happen to be there, so you become the recipient of the client's frustration and anger.

3. *Before responding, you take time to recognize that the client is angry at the situation, not at you. Therefore, there's no need for you to defend yourself.*

This last response works best. It enables you to stop your defense mechanism from kicking in. It's easier to do this than you think. It takes practice, but you can do it if you set your mind to it! As soon as you feel yourself getting uptight and feel the need to defend yourself, stop and analyze the situation. The customer is upset at your company or the situation—not at you. There is absolutely no need for you to defend yourself. Instead, you can concentrate on solving the client's problem. The client ends up happy and so do you—a win–win situation.

The correct approach is to concentrate on the client's problem, rather than on your own feelings.

You accomplish this by:

- taking notes while the person is talking;
- responding by paraphrasing to be sure that you understand the person's problem. This proves that you have been listening to what he or she is saying;
- asking questions.

Passing the buck, saying you're not responsible, or defending your company is not the answer. The customer doesn't care whether the mistake is yours or someone else's; he or she just wants you to remove the problem. You'll stay calmer if you don't take a defensive stance. Usually, when you've solved the problem, the client will say, "I'm sorry I yelled at you!"

DO YOUR MOODS CONTROL YOU?

Before you can tackle dealing with difficult people, it's essential that you have your own act together. Think of the last time you didn't feel in control during a trying situation. What happened to your self-esteem level? Most people find that their feeling of self-worth plummets after these kinds of encounters, so staying in control during difficult situations is essential for good mental health.

Do you have mood swings that affect what kind of day you have? Are you up one day, down the next—up one hour, down the next? Many times your mood depends on what's happening around you: Somebody snarls at you or gives you a mountainous job to do. You think, "Oh God, give me strength!" It's the little annoyances that can ruin your day, so if you can handle them constructively, you're certainly ahead of the game.

One method that can help you identify these kinds of situations is to be aware of your physical reactions, that is, what's happening to your body. The "flight or fight" response kicks in whenever we encounter difficult situations. Physical signs include tense muscles, gritted teeth or clenched jaw, rapid pulse, pounding heart, increased perspiration, shortness of breath, a rise in blood pressure, clammy skin, cold hands and feet, and/or rapid breathing. Whenever you identify these signs in yourself, stop for a split second and ask yourself "Am I reacting correctly—or am I overreacting to this situation?" You'll find that in about eight out of ten situations you've overreacted—given someone else control over the situation.

Too often, we let others control how we feel about ourselves. We allow them to give us bad or good days. We can attempt to change others' behavior, but we aren't always successful. However, we do have control over how we react to their behavior. My life changed when I realized that I could choose how I reacted when confronted with difficult situations. I could either take the bad feelings being handed to me by others or simply not take them. When I learned this basic technique, I found I had far more control over my moods. Gone were the rollercoaster mood swings of the past. Other people didn't decide what kind of day I'd have—I did! You, too, can have this control. Mind you, you will encounter exceptions, but many moods and reactions you *can* control. When you control the little difficulties, you're better equipped to handle the really big ones.

Picture this scene: You're driving to work, feeling pretty good about yourself and life. Suddenly, a car swerves in front of you, nearly causing a collision. You slam on the brakes (everything on the front seat goes flying) and hope for the best. Disaster averted by a margin of inches, you peel yourself off the steering wheel, scrunch over to pick things up off the floor and look for the car that cut you off. It has disappeared.

What's your first reaction—to rant and rave about rotten drivers? How long do you stay mad at the driver of the other car? And what good does it do? I've seen people vibrate at a fever pitch for hours, relating their experience to anyone who will listen.

After the car cut you off, you had two choices. You could stay upset about it, or admit you were in an emergency situation that you handled well and continue calmly driving to work.

If you *chose* to remain upset, you can't blame the other driver for it. What you do after something negative happens to you is *your* decision, not the other person's. If you allow someone else to upset you, you've made the wrong choice.

How do you react when a close friend or colleague says something that hurts your feelings? Do you withdraw into yourself and mull over the situation for a couple of weeks before you deal with it? Possibly the only thing that breaks the ice between you is that the other person notices your reaction and says, "What's wrong? You're so quiet." You may or may not respond honestly, mentioning the comment that hurt your feelings. Instead of spending this time in misery, learn to:

1. Immediately identify that you're hurt.
2. Right away, discuss your feelings with the person who caused the upset. You could say something like "That last comment was below the belt. Can you tell me why you made such a comment?" Or "Your last comment hurt my feelings. Did you mean it the way I heard it?"

Or does the following happen to you. Someone has done something really awful to you—and you don't care how long it takes you but you're going to pay them back! You know what this is—REVENGE! It feels good when we can pay someone back for a misdeed, but if you can't do so within a reasonable amount of time, let it go. If you analyze this situation, you'll realize that the other person has control over your life the entire time you're planning your revenge. In the meantime, you can't get on with your life and do constructive things. I've witnessed people still planning revenge ten years after their divorce. What a waste of energy! I've also observed that if you let it go and watch, you'll find that "what comes around goes around"—the person will be paid back for the misdeed without you having to waste your valuable energy.

Do you spend your time wailing "If only I'd . . ." or "I should have . . ."? What a waste of your life! Instead, concentrate on the present and the future—not the past.

We live in a guilt-ridden society. Others take glee in pointing out our faults. My philosophy is that if you've done your best, that's all you can expect of yourself. If you didn't succeed at something, you haven't failed—you've learned something. Do you feel guilty if you've made a mistake? Did you give your best effort? If so, the best way for you to deal with the situation (especially if someone else points out your mistake) is to say, "You're right—I did make a mistake. It won't happen again." So, don't feel guilty if you've made a mistake; instead learn from the experience and don't make the same mistake again.

Here's another example. You've worked very hard completing an assignment and are very proud of your accomplishment. You wait ... and *wait* for some kind of recognition from your supervisor. Is it likely to come? In many instances—no. You're more likely to hear about the small portion of the assignment you did wrong.

On top of it all, you're probably your own worst critic. There's a little twerp in all of us who is forever criticizing us, saying such things as, "Well, you goofed again! Can't you do anything right?"

Learn to stop criticizing yourself and start giving yourself positive reinforcement. If you've done a good job, you should mentally pat yourself on the back with such thoughts as "I'm really proud of how I did that job." Don't count on others to do this. If they do, think of their praise as "gravy"—but you don't need gravy on the potatoes every night, do you? Like too much gravy (which can make you swell up), too much praise can make you swell-headed. The person you should be trying to please is yourself. Never compete against the record of someone else. Just improve your own record of accomplishments.

The next time something like this happens to you, don't accept the negative feelings it causes. Blocking those feelings takes hard, concentrated effort on your part. Practice this skill until you automatically respond the way you want to. You may find yourself slipping back into your old defensive or retaliatory ways, but keep at it. If you do, you'll be able to keep your cool more often when under fire.

Whenever you're having any strong negative feeling, stop to evaluate whether the feeling is realistic or not.

Every day we're bombarded with negative situations. Examine the list below and determine which of these feelings you have NOT felt in the past month:

NEGATIVE FEELINGS

angry	hurt	guilty	anxious
depressed	frustrated	ignored	disappointed
ashamed	jealous	inferior	insecure
embarrassed	intimidated	rejected	nervous
distressed	concerned	flustered	humiliated
resentful	restricted	stupid	sad
dumb	suspicious	troubled	uneasy
tense	upset	uneasy	worried
agitated	remorseful	offended	hindered

Is it any wonder that many people have become negative-thinking? So, watch for the physical signs (which you will likely experience when you encounter people trying to instill any of the above negative feelings in you), and ask yourself whether you're overreacting. If you've determined that the feeling is not realistic, you've overreacted. This response could lag as much as ten minutes after the negative situation happened. Instead, turn off your negative reaction—let it go. If you find your mind constantly returning to these negative occurrences, remind yourself that you're giving someone else control over your life—and don't do it!

Ask yourself whether you're overreacting, or reacting reasonably to the situation. In performing this evaluation, you stay in charge of your emotions, and are therefore in control of the situation.

The Positive Approach

I'm sure there have been times when you've had a day where everything's gone wrong. You wish you could go back to bed (and it's only 10:00 a.m.). How you react to this kind of day often determines its outcome. Most people respond by saying, "Oh boy. It's going to be one of those days!" They expect the rest of the day to be as bad—and, of course, it is!

After three or four things have gone wrong in a day, have a talk with yourself. Instead of saying, "It's going to be one of those days," say,

"Thank goodness I got *that* over with." What you're doing is telling yourself that the rest of the day is going to be better. Try changing to a positive attitude when you're having a bad day and see if it doesn't turn things around.

How People Deal with Negative Feelings

Many people believe (incorrectly) that negative emotions are always dangerous and powerful. If they express these feelings openly, they tell themselves, they'll lose someone's love or provoke people's anger, boredom or dislike. They can't accept, either, that wanting to be liked by everybody all the time is an unrealistic goal.

Other people believe (also incorrectly) that it's "unhealthy" or "dishonest" to try to control how they express their feelings. They believe they have the right to let people know how they feel in any manner they choose, no matter what the circumstances—or the consequences.

Most people believe there are only two things they can do with bad emotions: (a) repress them or (b) express them in the form in which they experience them—that is, negatively. Most of us are also aware that both ways can be pretty destructive.

Temper tantrums. These are childish, inappropriate, uncontrolled expressions of anger that can be triggered by anything—some trivial recent event or something that took place long ago that has been festering for years. People who are prone to temper tantrums may deal with the minor irritations of day-to-day life by saying nothing at the time, then, when a chance remark acts as a trigger, erupting in a red flash of rage and lashing out at whoever is nearest. This fury has unfortunate consequences; the person feels terrible and others are alienated.

Sulking. Sulkers are ready to show they're in a bad mood but refuse to explain why. The "silent treatment" and "acting hurt" are variants of sulking.

Sarcasm. People who resort to sarcasm to express negative emotions are usually reluctant to confront the cause of their bad mood directly.

Logic versus Emotion: The Analytical Approach

If negative emotions are absorbed, they have to be released somehow. We have seen some of the instinctive ways people deal with them. Most of these reactions have negative consequences. The challenge is to find ways to deal with negative emotions constructively.

Two forces—logic and emotion—are at work throughout our lives. Often they push and pull in opposite directions. The one that prevails at any particular time will determine how we get along with others and may affect our level of achievement. It's easy to respond to situations with emotions rather than logic, but responding logically helps us deal constructively with difficult circumstances.

If it does not come naturally to you to behave logically when you're under stress, don't be discouraged. The ability to use logic to help resolve conflicts and problems can be developed. The first step is to gain some insight into the nature of the difficulty. You can do this by analyzing the situation, your feelings and your behavior. Armed with information from this analysis, you can then learn to take charge of your reactions instead of letting your instincts control you.

Here are two examples that show how the analytical approach could be useful.

1. Suppose you feel depressed for no other reason than because it's Monday morning. Do you phone in sick, or do you try to figure out what's wrong? When you analyze your reactions, you realize that you regularly feel up on Friday afternoon and down on Monday morning. If so, you may be one of the more than 80 percent of employed people who are in the wrong job. Do you let that depress you further, or do you do the logical thing and seriously consider looking for more suitable employment?

   When you consider that most of us spend ten hours a day, five days a week either getting ready for, traveling to or in the workplace, it's a shame that people don't spend more energy deciding what they would like to do with their lives. If you find yourself in the wrong job or occupation and decide to look for something you enjoy more, you could start by contacting a government-sponsored career center.

2. Or suppose you are under pressure to finish a job by 2:00 p.m., when your supervisor suddenly gives you an extra batch of work. Because your supervisor often does this, you find that you regularly have difficulty completing your allotted work on time. This makes you feel inadequate. On the other hand, you don't want to annoy your supervisor by saying no. Do you try to avoid saying no to your supervisor and end up at 2:00 p.m. having to say, "I'm sorry, boss, I didn't finish it yet"? Or do you say, "I won't have time to complete both this and the Jones report by 2:00 p.m. Which would you rather I do?"

In the first case, your supervisor is angry with you anyway because, by not speaking up, you have made it impossible to arrange for someone else to complete the report. You then complain, saying, "My job makes me feel that I'm under a lot of pressure."

In the second case, your analysis of the situation has made you realize that it is your supervisor's responsibility to help you set priorities. To ensure that this task can be done effectively, make sure you have a good idea of your present workload. Perhaps you have taken a time-management course to help you choose priorities. You keep "To do" lists, so you know exactly how much you can handle in a day, and you are careful to keep your supervisor informed of your workload.

Analyzing Stress

Certain physical and behavioral symptoms are associated with stress. Physical signs may include tense muscles, gritted teeth or clenched jaw, rapid pulse, pounding heart, increased perspiration, shortness of breath, a rise in blood pressure, clammy skin, cold hands and feet, sluggish digestion, rapid breathing, heightened sensitivity to noise and "racing" thoughts. Stress-related behavior may include impatience, restlessness, sudden rages or bouts of laughing or weeping, and a tendency to heightened emotion of all types. In some cases depression and apathy may also be reactions to stress.

Not all stress is bad. The heightened emotions and physical symptoms associated with stress can occur in response to pleasurable and exciting events—such as being promoted or falling in love. It's not stress in itself that's the problem, then, but negative stress—the kind that produces *dis*tress.

For example, most people assume that workaholics are unhappy, but that's not always true. There are two basic kinds of workaholic. There are those who love their jobs, and work hard and long because they receive pleasure from doing so. They're under stress but seldom suffer from real *dis*tress.

Other workaholics are motivated not by enthusiasm but by such things as

- competitive feelings;
- job pressures;
- budget cuts;
- family or relationship problems;
- financial problems.

Their stress becomes *dis*tress and they suffer because of it. We all know these people; they

- work all the time, often bringing work home in the evening and on the weekend—but are resentful about it;
- suffer from nervous disorders;
- don't eat or exercise right;
- never take time off from work when they're ill. (They're the ones who pass on the flu bug to the rest of the staff because they come in when they shouldn't);
- seldom spend time with their family;
- don't know how to relax, or play or simply "goof-off." (They often use competitive sports to relax.)

If you suspect you're a workaholic, the questionnaire that follows may give you further insight into whether your work is a source of positive or negative stress.

Are You a Workaholic?

Part A

	Yes	No
1. Are you always punctual for appointments?	____	____
2. Are you more comfortable when you're productive than idle?	____	____
3. Do you carefully organize your hobbies?	____	____
4. When you participate in recreational activities, is it mainly with work associates?	____	____
5. Even under pressure, do you usually take the extra time to make sure you have all the facts before you make a decision?	____	____
6. Are most of your friends in the same line of work as you?	____	____
7. Is most of your reading work-related?	____	____
8. Do you work late more frequently than your peers?	____	____
9. Do you talk shop over coffee or cocktails on social occasions?	____	____
10. Do your dreams center on work- or family-related conflicts?	____	____
11. Do you play as hard as you work?	____	____
12. Do you become restless on vacation?	____	____
13. Do your spouse and friends think of you as an easygoing person?	____	____

If you answered yes to the first twelve questions and no to question 13, you're a workaholic, all right; but keep in mind that this is not bad unless it's causing you distress. To find out if your workaholism is a source of negative stress, answer the questions in Part B.

Part B

	Yes	No
14. Do you seem to communicate better with your co-workers than with your spouse (or best friend)?	____	____
15. Are you better able to relax on Saturdays than on Sunday afternoons?	____	____
16. Do you take work to bed with you when you're home sick?	____	____
17. Are you usually very annoyed when others keep you waiting?	____	____
18. Do you wake up in the night worrying about business or family problems?	____	____
19. In competitive sports do you occasionally see your supervisor's face on the ball?	____	____
20. Is work sometimes a way of avoiding close relationships?	____	____
21. Do you usually plan every step of the itinerary of a trip in advance and become uncomfortable if plans go awry?	____	____
22. Do you enjoy small talk at a cocktail party or reception?	____	____

If you answered yes to questions 14 through 21 and no to question 22, you're probably not enjoying your long, hard hours of work.

If your distress keeps up long enough, the almost inevitable result will be burnout. To check for signs of burnout, ask yourself the following questions.

Do I:

- feel down or depressed most of the time?
- feel tired most of the time?
- have trouble eating and sleeping properly?
- feel there's no hope for improvement in my circumstances?
- complain constantly?

- feel that no one cares?
- feel upset, frustrated or angry most of the time?
- experience feelings of intense pressure and competition at work?
- feel that, no matter what I do, it won't be enough?
- fear that I'm going under any day now?

Stress becomes *dis*tress when we've been under pressure too long or the pressures of life become overwhelming. The first step in dealing with *dis*tress is to analyze all the sources of stress in your life to determine, first, which are positive and which are negative, and, second, which you can do something about and which you can't change. To do this, do the following exercise, answering as accurately as you can. Write down your answers, don't just go through the exercise mentally.

1. On a sheet of paper, list everything that's causing you stress. (Leave space between each stressor.) Try to identify at least five stressors.
2. On a scale of 1 to 10 (10 being the highest), determine the level of each stressor.
3. Determine if the stressor is positive (a wedding, a promotion, a new baby, a new job) or negative (rudeness, driving in rush-hour traffic).
4. Record the feelings you have when in the stressful situation (anger, frustration, happiness, fear) next to each stressor.
5. Identify which part of your life is most affected by each negative stressor (family, social, business/work).
6. Then, for each negative stressor, determine whether:
   a. you *do* have the power to alleviate the problem. Put the word "do" next to the item; or
   b. you *don't* have the power to change the situation. It's beyond your control—there's nothing you can do about it. Put the word "don't" next to the item.

Techniques for Reducing Negative Stress

Once you have identified the sources of negative stress in your life and have determined which of them you could do something about, you're well on the way to obtaining relief from the worst pressures.

Your analysis should then be followed by two more steps:

7. If you don't have the power to do something about a source of negative stress, forget about it. Mentally throw the problem in the garbage can and don't waste any more precious energy thinking about it.
8. If you do have the power to change the situation, think about what you are going to do about it. Draw up a plan of action.

Taking these steps, you put the Serenity Prayer (written by Reinhold Niebuhr) into practice:

"God grant me the serenity to accept the things I cannot change, the courage to change the things I can, and the wisdom to know the difference."

One of my seminar participants identified the following problem: "My personal annoyance is rush-hour traffic. Almost every day, I get into a bad mood watching the dumb things other drivers do." This is probably one of the things in your life that you have no control over. What you do have control over is your reaction to it. Drive defensively. Remind yourself not to get upset. Use your energy constructively, by tuning in to your favorite radio station or playing a tape you enjoy. You might consider traveling earlier or later to miss traffic jams.

SIX BEHAVIOR STYLES

Here are six basic behavioral styles and the behaviors that go along with them:

ASSERTIVE BEHAVIOR

- Respect for oneself—expressing one's needs and defending one's rights.
- Respect for the other person's needs and rights.

PASSIVE BEHAVIOR

- No respect for oneself.
- Not expressing one's needs or defending one's rights.

AGGRESSIVE BEHAVIOR

- No respect for the other person's needs and rights.

PASSIVE RESISTANCE

These are passive people who are trying to become more assertive in their behavior. They mutter and sigh a lot and play manipulative games to get their way. They've not learned to ask up-front for what they want.

Joey: Mom, can you drive me to school today?

His mother had her morning planned. It was a beautiful day, and Joey as usual had been fooling around and now was late leaving for school.

Mom: Joey, I've driven you twice this week ...

Joey: Oh Mom ... please?

Mom (letting out a big sigh): Oh, all right!

Her body language and speech say, "Just look at the sacrifices I make for you. If you loved me more, you'd appreciate me more!"

INDIRECT AGGRESSION

These people exhibit behavior that is between being assertive and obviously aggressive. They use subtle, underhanded ways to get their way, such as sabotage, sarcasm, the silent treatment and gossip. For example:

Don: "My wife wants me to clean the basement this weekend. I'm going to give it a stab, but won't clean it to her standards. Then maybe she won't expect me to do that job again." (Sabotage).

Jane: "I see you finally made the decision to get your hair cut in a style that suits you." (Sarcasm).

Linda hadn't spoken to her husband Bill for four days following an argument. They hadn't resolved the issue, and Bill had tried several times to get her to talk about the problem—she refused. (The silent treatment).

Jill: Did you hear about Carmen's husband ... he was picked up for drunk driving last night. (Gossip).

PASSIVE-AGGRESSIVE

These people have a pathological reaction to authority and those they perceive to be in positions of authority. They have a tendency to blow up unexpectedly, keeping others off balance because their behavior often doesn't follow the usual pattern. Normally a person shows signs of frustration before losing his or her temper—these people do it "out of the blue" when it's completely unexpected. They gain the trust of others, then stab them in the back. This causes others to use caution when dealing with them, but they can be so charming that they worm their way into our good graces, obtaining our trust. Then they repeat their pattern. We must always expect the unexpected with these people and be on guard, anticipating a repeat of their destructive behavior. See Chapter 2 for more details about their behavior.

APPROACHES TO CONFLICT RESOLUTION

We have seen that many conflicts and resentments arise because people feel either that they have to defend themselves against an aggressor or that they have inadvertently taken advantage of a too-passive person. The ability to behave assertively rather than aggressively or passively can significantly reduce the level of conflict and stress in your life; however, conflicts cannot be avoided entirely.

The basic approaches to resolving conflicts are:

1. *Competition.* One person or group wins, the other loses.
2. *Accommodation.* One person refuses even to state his or her wishes, but simply goes along with the other's statements or demands.
3. *Compromise/Collaboration.* Each person recognizes the other's rights. Each may need to yield on some points, but it is understood that the solution must take into account the needs and wishes of both.

There are no competitive feelings in the last approach. Instead, there is a feeling of cooperation or camaraderie among the participants. This attitude uses each person's talents and recognizes each person's rights.

THE WAY TO WIN ARGUMENTS

Nobody likes to lose an argument. Here are clues to how you might win your next one.

1. Ask for time to think things over. Take this opportunity to allow both of you to calm down.
2. Pay attention to your body's reaction. Has the fight-or-flight instinct been triggered? Take a deep breath to increase your oxygen intake to your brain so you can analyze your situation more clearly.

3. Don't snap at the person. You may regret a fast retort which may have lasting repercussions.
4. Determine what it is you want that you're not getting. Should you be willing to negotiate more—to give in a little—so you can both win?
5. If the other person has "lost it," don't negotiate until calm returns. Adopting a quiet manner is always your best approach.
6. Wait until the other person is willing to listen to your side of the story. Make sure you're listening carefully to his or her side of the story.
7. Make sure the other person knows you're listening. Use paraphrasing on a regular basis to confirm that what you heard is what was said.
8. The other person doesn't seem to be listening to what you have to say. Insist that you be listened to. Say, *"I've made a point of listening carefully to what you have to say. Can I count on you to do the same for me?"*
9. Ask, *"What do you want me to do?"* Clarify that you know what the other person wants. Listen to the answer and confirm or correct.
10. State what you want, clearly and sequentially. Again, be willing to negotiate.
11. Once an agreement is reached, summarize the particulars and go over pertinent areas again to reconfirm your understanding.

AGREE TO DISAGREE

There are times when you'll find yourself in a conversation with others and recognize that you're on opposite sides of the issue. For instance: abortion, gun control, politics, religion, euthanasia. Neither of you will budge an inch, and both parties become more and more upset because the other can't see things from their perspective.

This is especially trying for people who have great respect and admiration for each other. It's important to recognize that no two people (no matter how close they are) can think the same way about every issue in life. Others are not traitors (as you might feel they are) should their views differ from yours.

Whenever you find yourself in this kind of situation say, *"You're entitled to your opinion and so am I. It's obvious that we're never going to agree on this issue, so let's agree to disagree, and not talk about this in the future."* If the other person insists on continuing with the argument, refuse to participate in the discussion. If the issue comes up later, remind the other person that you will not budge from your opinion, so it's unwise to get heated up about the issue again.

BEING CONSTRUCTIVE

Of course it is sometimes necessary to discuss people's mistakes—in other words, to criticize them. Criticism can be either *destructive*—just making the person feel worthless—or *constructive*—offering specific suggestions for improvement. When criticizing others, always suggest ways to improve the person's behavior. Don't simply apply labels such as dumb, stupid, lazy, sloppy, ignorant, uncaring. People don't know how to correct such faults, and using such terms just provokes retaliation in the person receiving the comment.

Think about the last rip-snorting argument you had with someone. Did you label the *person*, or did you play fair and discuss the person's *behavior*?

For example, you could say: "John, how could you do such a dumb thing?" That's labeling John without giving him any information about how to stop being "dumb."

Or you could say: "John, you didn't spend much time preparing your report, did you? It turned out to be useless, and I had to do it over again." That's discussing his behavior and giving him specific information about how he can change it.

In an argument, if you find yourself labeling someone, please apologize. Say, "I'm sorry. You didn't deserve that. What I meant was ...."

You can then discuss the behavior that offended you, using the feedback technique.

If people label you, ask for specific reasons why they have given you the label. Remember you have the choice of accepting or not accepting the criticism.

We can decide not to allow people to hurt us. A co-worker may betray us, gossip about us, or try to give us guilt trips. It's not easy to forgive this behavior. We may feel that we're letting ourselves down if we forgive others too easily. We may feel we should wait for them to do something to mend the rift. We may be tempted to dwell to an unhealthy extent on the injury we feel others have done us.

In many cases, however, forgiving is the only thing that will mend and heal. Forgiving can actually lead to a renewed relationship.

You may say, "That's easy for you to say! Your co-worker didn't gossip behind your back and pass on untrue information about you!"

Here's what you can do to mend the rift. Stop pretending that you like the person. Acknowledge to yourself that you are angry, and examine why. Then be direct with the other person, telling him or her frankly what has offended you. Keep in mind, however, that the person is only human, and that we all make mistakes. Then make a conscious decision to forgive and forget. (You have to mean it.) Once you forgive the person, you can get on with your life.

Many people don't agree with this approach. They believe that forgiving wrongdoers just lets them off the hook—it's too easy on them. In reality, however, holding a grudge ties the injured party to the wrongdoer. Anger and hate use up energy that should be spent positively in picking up the pieces.

I found that I could get on with my life when I forgave others for injuries done to me. Ironically, in my case, all these people have subsequently had problems resulting directly from their own hurtful behavior. For instance, one boss I had was afraid that I might be after his job. He made my life a living hell for months, which caused terrible stress and health problems for me. I finally had to admit defeat and look for work elsewhere. That man is now bouncing from one job to another, each at a lower level than the one before. He leaves behind a string of former co-workers who despise him.

Accepting Compliments

Many of us have difficulty receiving compliments graciously. We discount or refuse to accept them, countering with such comments as: "Oh, I could have done better" or "This old rag?"

If you don't accept compliments graciously, what are you telling the person giving you the compliment? You're implying that he or she is insincere or has poor judgment. You are repaying a warm fuzzy (a good feeling) with a cold prickly (a bad feeling). Remember this the next time you discount a compliment.

Dealing with Language Barriers

Until they become completely fluent in English, people who speak English as a second language normally go through the following process:

Stage 1. They hear what you say in English.
Stage 2. They translate what you've said into their first language.
Stage 3. They construct their answer in their first language.
Stage 4. They mentally translate the answer into English.
Stage 5. They reply to you in English.

You can see that this process takes time, so if you're conversing with people whose second language is English, try to:

1. Use simple, ordinary language. You can't expect them to learn jargon or technical language right away.
2. Watch their body language. If they frown, you may have lost them. Repeat what you said, using simpler language.
3. Allow them time to interpret what you've said. The "pregnant pause" between the end of your speech and the beginning of their response may be necessary for complete understanding on their part.

Sometimes, no matter what you do, you may find it impossible to understand what someone is saying to you. Whenever possible, try to find someone who speaks the person's language. If that's not possible, ask the person to bring along someone (perhaps a child or a relative) who can act as an interpreter.

If this is a recurring problem, check government offices to see if they have interpreters available to translate. Refer the caller to this service.

Catch yourself if you have guilt feelings. If you've done everything you can to understand the person, you have no reason to accept any guilt feelings.

In the past I had the misfortune of having to deal with a receptionist who had a very strong accent. I couldn't understand what she was saying, and I don't think she could understand me. This problem continued for about two weeks. I wasn't able to conduct business properly with the company. I finally decided to do something, and asked to speak to the office manager. I explained my dilemma this way:

"I have a problem and I need your help in solving it. Several times in the past two weeks I've called your company and have had difficulty understanding what your new receptionist was saying. Have others complained to you about this? You may be losing clients because of it."

She admitted she had heard rumblings from co-workers in the office, but said I was the first complaint from outside the company. She assured me that she would solve the problem. The next time I called the company, a new person answered the phone. If I hadn't complained, the situation might have gone on much longer, with clients lost for this company along the way.

WHAT KIND OF PERSON ARE YOU?

From the information given below, choose the type that most closely represents your behavior pattern. Then analyze the information to determine where your difficult person fits.

TYPE	STRENGTHS	WEAKNESSES
A.	Direct	Brow-beats
	Outgoing	Domineering
	Up-front	Restless
	Stimulating	Impatient
	People-skilled	Pushy
	Persuasive	Manipulative
	Risk-taker	Grating
	Competitive	Reactive
	Self-assured	Controlling

These people are spontaneous, are often employed in sales, are people-people. They want respect from others. Others may feel they're aggressively competitive in their pursuit of what they want. They dislike others who lack enthusiasm, keep them waiting, or are indecisive or rigid, by-the-book people. They love attention, sense of achievement, and crave recognition, adventure and excitement.

TYPE	STRENGTHS	WEAKNESSES
B.	Practical	Uncaring
	Ambitious	Critical
	Efficient	Frugal
	Methodical	Unyielding
	Direct	Aloof
	Results-oriented	Uncompromising
	Conventional	Distant
	Resolute	Insistent
	Determined	Stubborn
	Organized	Inflexible
	Dependable	Inaccessible

These people make good entrepreneurs and directors. They like to direct and take charge of things. They're task-oriented, and must always win. They hate emotional people, and ambiguity, disrespect and laziness in others. They like others to be controlled and loyal, keep a fast pace, and like responsibility.

TYPE	STRENGTHS	WEAKNESSES
C.	Team-oriented	Too empathetic
	Warm	Indecisive
	Faithful	Unreasonable
	Enthusiastic	Defenseless
	Co-operative	Wishy-washy
	Approachable	Subjective
	Trusting	Hesitant
	Sensitive	Irrational
	Good listener	Vulnerable
	Good friend	Push-over
	Likes change	Passive
	Outgoing	Pleasing others
	Ambassador	Walked-on

These people are often in the service industry (hospitality, health care, transportation, social services) because they have a strong desire to help others. They hold in stress and store it away—seldom put themselves first. They're protective of the underdog, want everyone to love them, and are often passive in their behavior. They dislike insensitive, argumentative, insincere or egotistical people. They like others who are warm, kind and caring.

TYPE	STRENGTHS	WEAKNESSES
D.	Rigid	Procrastinates
	Meticulous	Perfectionist
	Accurate	Unsociable
	Inhibited	Uninteresting
	Painstaking	Brooding
	Sensible	Bashful
	Serene	Passive
	High standards	Hates change
	Avoids risks	Monotonous

These are more detail-oriented than people-people. They enjoy working alone, often in accounting, technical or engineering fields. They dislike people who are fakes or are overly assertive, careless or arrogant. They like those who are perfectionists, consistent, informed, practical, do good work, and are easy to get along with.

HOW TO WORK WITH OTHER PERSONALITY TYPES

If you're in a working or personal relationship with someone of this style, here are a few things that may be helpful to remember.

If your supervisor or manager is from one of these types, consider these guidelines:

A. Type

- Give praise, credit and recognition regularly.
- Be sociable with them.
- Treat them as if what they're doing is important.
- Encourage them to use their creative abilities.
- If they're hyperactive, rechannel their energies—help them choose priorities.

A. Type

- Be sociable with them.
- Give them lots of credit
- Help them interact with others.
- Help see things in a realistic light.
- Show enthusiasm and excitement.
- Be up-front in communication.
- Feed their ego.
- Be open and friendly.
- Be outgoing, not shy with them.

B. Type

- Give them as much control as possible.
- Give loose supervision—lots of rope.
- Make them feel important.
- Utilize their efficient, practical, ambitious nature.
- Use their organizational abilities.
- Respect their conventional values and methods.
- Be flexible in accepting their way of doing things.

B. Type

- Document everything.
- Be results-oriented.
- Respect their authority.
- Give them challenges.
- Follow rules and regulations.
- Be punctual. Keep to the point.
- Be buffer between them and other employees.
- Help them see other alternative ways of doing things.

C. Type

- Don't get upset with their need to have everyone like them.
- Treat others even more fairly when in their presence.
- Be up-front in your dealings with them.
- Give them opportunities to mingle with others.
- Have patience with their indecisive behavior.

C. Type

- Show you're interested in them and what they do.
- Offer support
- Freely express thoughts and ideas.
- Be a team player, willing to compromise.
- Help communicate with others.
- Set your own objectives and complete them.

D. Type

- Listen to their ideas.
- Help them set deadlines.
- Give them room to do the job their way.
- Use logic and facts in discussions.
- Show respect.

D. Type

- Give detailed hard facts and data.
- Acknowledge their proficiency.
- Be consistent.
- Document ideas giving facts to back up.
- Offer new ideas and approaches.

Now, list your difficult people:

NAME   PERSONALITY TYPE

1. _____

2. _____

3. _____

NAME   PERSONALITY TYPE

4. _____

   a) What could you change in your approach to them that would
      improve the situation?
   b) When dealing with this person I will remember the following:

1. _____

   _____

2. _____

   _____

3. _____

   _____

4. _____

   _____

INTROVERT, EXTROVERT, PERSONALITY TYPES

It's important to analyze where your difficult people fit in relation to
their wants, needs and desires. Analyze your difficult persons to see
how you can more effectively deal with their difficult behavior by evaluating where they fit into the following three categories:

Extreme Introvert: This person is extremely careful, is contemplative
and analytical, leans toward perfectionism, and can work doggedly at
detailed work. Introverts tend to be "cerebral" and are concerned with
affairs of the mind rather than a lot of physical activity.

Extreme Extrovert: This person is more action-oriented, prefers to get started quickly, deciding on details along the way (or ignoring them altogether, thinking someone else will take care of them). Extroverts may get many things started, but leave some details unfinished.

Combination Introvert/Extrovert: This person combines some attributes of both the introvert and extrovert and is a balance of the two extremes. Their individual actions would tell you which phase they are in at that time.

Common Ways Extreme Introverts Feel and Behave:	*Common Ways Extreme Extroverts Feel and Behave:*
1. Don't like to lend things to others. They'll do it, but with much hesitancy and caution.	Lend money and possessions readily.
2. Would rather make a report in writing than give it orally.	Fluent talkers; can give reports better orally than in writing.
3. Can be very blunt and straightforward.	Usually careful not to be outspoken or hurt others' feelings.
4. Are more reserved in their laughter or other displays of feelings and emotion.	Laugh readily.
5. Become embarrassed quite easily.	Hard to embarrass.
6. Are very careful with their personal possessions—clothes, tools, car, home and yard. Keep things looking nice and in good order.	Don't take care of personal possessions.
7. Are quite uncomfortable speaking or performing before an audience and avoid it as much as possible.	Are natural public speakers who are at ease in front of a crowd.

8. Are slow in action and decision-making.	Make decisions quickly.
9. Considered perfectionists by many. Write and rewrite until everything's perfect.	Are quick in their actions. Seldom rewrite letters or give attention to detail.
10. Are cautious in forming new relationships.	Make new friends quickly.
11. Though not generally talkative, they enjoy a good debate or argument.	Don't like to argue.
12. Are chronic worriers.	Aren't worriers.
13. Are quite concerned and deliberate about most routine decisions.	Aren't bothered by details of what to wear, what to eat, where to go, etc.
14. Are very sensitive about comments made about them.	Aren't very concerned about what's said about them.
15. Resent autocratic commands from others.	Accept orders as a matter of course.
16. Can be extreme in religion, politics and other social issues.	Are usually moderate in their views in relation to religion, politics and other social issues.
17. Tend to struggle alone with problems.	Don't hesitate to ask for help in solving problems.
18. Are quite comfortable working alone, rather than as a member of a team.	Would rather work with others than alone.
19. Enjoy and need praise and recognition, but won't ask for it.	Make their own opportunities for praise.
20. Tend to be suspicious.	Aren't suspicious of others' motives.

21. Are more moody than a strong extrovert.	Are in about the same mood at all times.
22. Enjoy work requiring precision and attention to detail.	Prefer work where details are not important.
23. Prefer intellectual pursuits.	Prefer athletics to books and "high brow" activities.
24. Daydream a lot and think about what might have been or what is yet to come.	Are not great planners—take things as they come.
25. Are extremely conscientious and berate themselves for less than perfect performance.	Are risk-takers and gamblers—seldom worry about the consequences.

STYLES OF BEHAVIOR AND THEIR EFFECTS

To a large extent your ability to deal *constructively* with stress, anger and difficult situations depends on the *style of behavior* you most readily adopt.

How Passive People Feel about Themselves

People who normally use passive behavior likely feel:

- Angry—They *know* others take advantage of them.
- Frustrated—They seldom get their way.
- Withdrawn—They believe nobody listens to them.
- Insecure and inferior—They lack self-esteem and self-confidence, are unaware of their abilities, and are reluctant to try new things for fear of failing.

- Anxious—They feel they have little control over their lives.
- Defeated—They believe it's no use trying; they won't get what they want anyway.
- Unable to acknowledge feelings—They hide feelings of fear and inadequacy by pretending everything's all right.
- Liable to put themselves down—have difficulty accepting even the simplest compliment and tend to underestimate the value of what they do.
- Lacking in energy—Their zest for living is missing. They're usually doing things that others want them to do, rather than what *they* themselves want.

These people believe they're not okay, but you are okay.

How Aggressive People Feel about Themselves

People who normally use aggressive behavior likely feel:

- Powerful (in the short run)—They enjoy having people scurry and rush to do what they say.
- Guilty (eventually)—They know they're taking advantage of others.
- Threatened—They constantly let others know how good, intelligent, strong, etc., they are. They do this because others may learn they aren't really that good underneath their veneer. They attempt to make themselves feel important by putting others down.
- Right—They are convinced that the only ideas worth listening to are their own.
- Critical—They blame others when things go wrong.
- Lonely—Their aggression isolates them from everyone around them.
- Excessively energetic—They expend energy in the wrong direction, doing destructive rather than constructive things.

These people feel that they're okay, but you're not okay. Those who hit the outer edge of aggressive behavior (criminals) believe that they're not okay, but you're not okay either.

How Assertive People Feel about Themselves

People who normally use assertive behavior likely feel:

- Positive—They approach every new task or idea with a positive rather than a negative attitude.
- Calm—They're at peace with themselves and others.
- Enthusiastic—They complete tasks with zest and feel they'll succeed at them.
- Proud—They accomplish what they do without stealing ideas from others or climbing over others. They can take full credit for what they achieve.
- Honest—When they give their word that they'll do something, they do it, so others believe in them.
- Direct—They don't play manipulative games to get what they want. They deal up front in situations, and usually succeed at what they attempt.
- Confident—They take risks, but know their limitations. They know that it's okay to be wrong sometimes and are ready to learn from their mistakes.
- Satisfied—They know where they're going and how they're going to get there, so they usually attain their goals.
- In control—They seldom have mood swings that adversely affect their communication with and behavior toward others.
- Able to acknowledge feelings—They can explain to others what unpleasant behavior is doing to them.
- Respect for others—They recognize that others have needs and rights just as they do.
- Energetic—Their energy is directed toward achieving their goals.

These people feel that they're okay, and you're okay too.

Consequences of These Behavioral Styles

It's helpful to know how others are likely to react to you when you use different behavioral styles.

PASSIVE BEHAVIOR

Passive behavior can make others feel aggressive. People may shun someone who gives in again and again to their wishes. They don't like the guilty feelings they have when passive people allow themselves to be taken advantage of.

For example, Sarah was responsible for ensuring that the receptionist in the office (Judy) had someone to take over her duties during coffee, lunch and bathroom breaks. There were four employees on the list that Sarah could call on for this duty. Several of them were sick or couldn't spare the time one week, so Mary had to cover for Judy all that week. This made Mary get behind in her own work, and she had to work overtime two days that week.

The same problem existed the next two weeks, and Sarah had to rely on Mary again. Mary willingly worked the second week. Sarah felt terrible asking her to cover the post the third week, but, grudgingly, Mary again agreed.

From then on, every time Sarah saw Mary, she felt guilty. She realized that, although she was normally an assertive person, she felt as though she had taken advantage of Mary (had acted aggressively) and as a consequence felt guilty. To combat this guilty feeling, she avoided Mary and didn't have normal contact with her.

Mary helped Sarah out because she wanted Sarah to like her, but ended up with a negative reaction (exactly what she tried not to do). Many passive people have this unexpected reaction to their "good deeds" and wonder what they've done wrong or how they may have offended others.

Dealing with passive people can also make others feel:

- Irritated—They wish you'd stand up for yourself and make your own decisions.
- Withdrawn—They avoid you because your negative attitude makes it difficult for them to maintain their own positive attitude.
- Superior—They lose respect for you as a person, because you aren't willing to stand up for what you believe in.
- Tired—They waste valuable energy dealing with their negative reactions to you.

AGGRESSIVE BEHAVIOR

Aggressive behavior can make others feel:

- Angry and threatened—They resent your unfair tactics.
- Frustrated—They waste valuable energy defending themselves from your abusive ways.
- Withdrawn—They avoid you because when you're around, they feel they must be ready to defend themselves.
- Anxious and defensive—They can't relax because they're preparing for the next attack.
- Resentful—They resent the power you seem to have over them.
- Hurt—They can't help being affected by your put-downs, even if they know your comments are undeserved.
- Humiliated—They don't enjoy being corrected or made to appear foolish in public.
- Tired—They waste valuable energy preparing for what you're going to throw at them next.

ASSERTIVE BEHAVIOR

Assertive behavior can make others feel:

- Positive—They sense that you will be pleased if they succeed.
- Secure—They trust you, because you let them know where they stand with you by offering constant feedback.
- Cooperative—They respond to your straightforward positive behavior by trying to help you.
- Respectful—They reciprocate the respect you show for their needs and rights.
- Energetic—They're able to use their energy constructively because there's no game-playing.

Who Wins?

Do assertive people usually achieve their goals? Yes, because their aim is for both sides to win. They believe in equality and are willing to negotiate.

Do passive people usually achieve their goals? No, because they seldom have goals in the first place. They expect others to look after them.

Do aggressive people usually achieve their goals? Sometimes, in the short run, but they often face antagonism and retaliation later.

You are now equipped with some basic insights into human behavior—your own and that of others. You will be able to switch off your defense mechanism when faced with negative comments and actions from others. The tool that will allow you to make effective use of these insights is your ability to communicate well with the people you encounter. In the next two chapters, you will learn how to deal with manipulators who use the above behaviors and learn specific communication skills you'll require for dealing with difficult people.

2

BASIC COMMUNICATION SKILLS

There are many skills that will help you deal with difficult people. If you find that you're often misunderstood, or that you misunderstand others too often, such skills are a must for you to practice and use.

PARAPHRASING

Paraphrasing means: to express meaning in other words; to rephrase; to give a message in another form; to amplify a message.

We normally use paraphrasing for simple things such as repeating telephone numbers when taking a message. If you simply repeat the person's message—that's parroting. If you ask yourself what the person means, and ask for confirmation of your understanding of their message—that's paraphrasing. Of the two methods, paraphrasing is much more effective.

The use of paraphrasing is essential when two people are conversing at any time. Unfortunately, when information isn't clear to us, we often make assumptions. We don't confirm with other people that what we *thought* they said was what they really meant us to understand.

You are receiving instructions on how to get to someone's house. You neglected to use paraphrasing to confirm that you have understood the directions, and you end up completely lost. Sound familiar?

Here's an example of two people talking but not understanding each other:

Bill:　　Jim didn't get that job he wanted.
Jennie:　He didn't get the job he wanted?
Bill:　　Yeah, and he's really upset about it.

In this conversation, Jennie thought she was using paraphrasing, but all she was doing was parroting what Bill said. Instead, she should have asked herself what Bill's statement *meant* to her. Some of her assumptions could have been:

- Jim asked for too much money.
- He was overqualified for the position.
- He was underqualified for the position.
- He blew the interview.
- Someone else was better than he.
- He's probably better suited to a different career.

If she had determined what the statement meant to her (Jim blew the interview) and had used paraphrasing, the earlier conversation would have been more like this:

Bill:　　Jim didn't get that job he wanted.
Jennie:　You mean he blew the interview?
Bill:　　Oh no, he learned that they had already chosen someone else for the position before he applied.
Jennie:　I'm sorry to hear that.
Bill:　　Yeah, and he's really upset about it.

You can see the difference between these two sets of conversations. In the first conversation, Bill and Jennie do not confirm their personal beliefs with each other. Bill believes that Jennie knows that Jim didn't get the job because they had someone else chosen for the position. Jennie, on the other hand, believes that Bill has confirmed her belief that Jim blew the interview. This is why problems occurred later: in a conversation with another friend, Jennie stated that both she and Bill agreed that Jim had blown the interview. She honestly believed that she was speaking the truth to her friend.

This kind of problem arises in many conversations. Ask for more information if you're not sure what a person means, or use paraphrasing to bring out discrepancies. You probably use this technique already but haven't been aware of it. If anyone has ever said to you, "No, that's not what I meant," you've already used paraphrasing and maybe didn't even know it! Use it often; it lessens communication problems.

It's also an excellent tool to use when clients are angry at something. If you write down details of the situation you're trying to correct, you're less likely to be spending your energy defending yourself. When the client has given all the information you need to solve the problem, use paraphrasing to make sure he or she knows you understand. The client will likely calm down and give you the opportunity to help.

Using Paraphrasing in Training Others

If you've had the responsibility of training others, you've probably had to explain more than once how to do something. Paraphrasing is a very effective tool to use when training others, especially if they're lazy listeners. To help them retain their training, do the following:

1. Give short, sequential instructions.
2. State, "To make sure that I was clear in my instructions to you, could you please explain what you're going to do?"
3. If the trainee is unable to recite the steps, repeat the instructions.
4. Again ask the trainee to recite the steps he or she will take to complete the task.

You'll find that trainees' listening skills will improve immeasurably when you use this technique. They'll know that when you train them to do anything new, there'll be a test to see if they've listened properly, and you'll find that giving instructions will be much easier in the future.

Do, however, remember that the onus is on you to make your instructions clear. Avoid such questions as:

- "Do you understand?" (People can just answer yes to this. You want to double-check by having them repeat the instructions back to you.)
- "Explain what I want you to do." (This is too overbearing. It will just put people's backs up.)
- "Did you catch that?" (This sounds like a put-down. People will resent the implication that they are stupid.)

If you think people might have misunderstood you, it's much better to make the problem yours. You can accomplish this by saying something like:

- "Let's see if I've been clear in my instructions to you."

You could then ask if they have any questions.

SENSORY LANGUAGE

When we say two people have "rapport" we usually mean their relationship is harmonious—they are able to get into someone else's world. We can enhance this rapport by determining the other person's primary sensory language. Most of us are a mixture of all three, but one usually stands out as being the primary sensory language.

People process information in different ways. They are primarily visual, auditory or kinesthetic (muscular movement) in the way they process information. Each type uses distinctive words that reflect his or her preference. To create rapport with people, listen to find out their primary mode, then mirror their language. Here are some examples:

The visual person might say:
  "I get the picture,"
  "I see what you mean" or
  "Let me see what the job looks like."
  "I see what you mean" or
  "My perception is . . ."

Auditory people use such phrases as:
> *"That sounds good to me."*
> *"I hear what you're saying,"*
> *"That rings a bell."*
> *"I hear you loud and clear."*
> *"She's not in tune with me"* or
> *"Let me explain how this works."*

Typical phrases for kinesthetic would be:
> *"Show me how to do this."*
> *"That doesn't feel right."*
> *"Hold on."*
> *"I'm comfortable with that."*
> *"I'll give you a feel for the job."*
> *"I grasp what you're saying."*
> *"That's a rough problem"* or
> *"You have a heavy task."*

1. Determine your primary sensory language.
2. Determine the primary sensory language of the people you deal with.
3. What changes can you make to communicate on the wave length of your difficult people?

Those who are responsible for training others have probably thrown their hands up in the air at times, when their information seems to go in one ear and out the other with some learners. Many people require constant repetition of instructions. This type of person may be a poor listener.

Information has a better chance of being "locked in" when trainers use a variety of training methods. These could include visual aids such as movies, slides or flip charts. To help trainees further "lock in" the training, see that they use the training as soon as possible. Keep in mind that trainees retain:

- 10 percent of what they read (handouts, manuals);
- 20 percent of what they hear (have explained to them);
- 30 percent of what they see done (demonstrations);
- 50 percent of what they read, hear and see done;
- 70 percent of what they read, hear, see done, and explain to someone else;

- 90 percent of what they read, hear, see done, explain to someone else and do themselves.

So you can see that the more sensory language methods you use, the better the training is retained.

People pass through four definite stages when learning something new. These stages are:

1. *Unconscious incompetence*—You aren't even aware that you lack the skill. For example, you may not even have known that the skill of paraphrasing existed.
2. *Conscious incompetence*—You're aware that you lack the skill. For example, before you learned how to use a computer you knew you couldn't use a computer.
3. *Conscious competence*—You know the techniques of the skill but have to stop and think before you react. ("Do I put the disk in first or turn the computer on first?")
4. *Unconscious competence*—The skill is now well established and automatic. You probably don't even think about what you're doing when you use the computer—you're on "automatic pilot."

It takes six weeks to "lock in" how to do something new, and up to three months to "lock in" doing something a different way than you used to.

These following elements are all part of the communication process:

- What I want to say/think I'm saying.
- What I actually say.
- What others think they hear.
- What others want to reply/think they're replying.
- What others actually reply.
- What I think I hear them say.

Different Interpretations of Words

Many words mean different things to different people. For example, if I invited you to my home for dinner tomorrow, when would you come?

Would it be at noon or one o'clock, or at five, six, seven or eight o'clock? Some people have *dinner* (the main meal of the day) at midday, others in the evening.

If I asked people from Alaska and Florida to describe a blizzard, do you think their descriptions would be the same? Of course not—because each person has a different experience of what this word means. (And a teenager might describe a blizzard as an ice cream treat that you eat!)

Male and Female Interpretations

Unfortunately, the simple act of communicating with one another can lead to confused messages, or messages being missed entirely. This is especially true when it comes to communication between men and women. It's no wonder there's conflict, when they interpret the same conversation in different ways. This is because of the different conversational styles of men and women.

Many examples will stereotype male/female responses. There are many exceptions to the examples I've identified. Analyze how you feel or respond to situations; compare them to those described, and decide if you need to change anything in your communication style.

As women grow up, talk is the thread from which relationships are woven. They develop and maintain friendships by exchanging secrets, and regard talking as the cornerstone of friendships. Men bond as intensely as women, but their friendships are based more on doing things together and don't require talk to cement relationships. Men converse to negotiate status; women to create rapport. Men are comfortable telling people what to do; women don't like to pull rank, so request, rather than demand (which leads the men to believe they have the right to accept or refuse the woman's request).

When conversing, women face each other directly, with eyes anchored on each other's face. Men sit at angles to each other and look elsewhere in the room—periodically glancing at each other—and often mirror each other's body movements. Men's tendency to face away from them when conversing gives women the impression that the men aren't listening to them, when in fact they are. The only times men will really look for any length of time at the person who's speaking are when they're trying to evaluate whether the speaker is lying or not; the speaker is hostile and they may have to take defensive action; or they're evaluating an attractive woman. In this last case, they'll glance over the woman's body while listening to her comments. This is highly distracting to the female speaker because the man's eyes mirror that he's not really listening to what she's saying, but rather sizing her up as a woman.

Another habit that gives women the impression men aren't listening is that they switch topics more often. Women tend to talk at length about one topic; men tend to jump from topic to topic. When a woman expresses her point of view, her female listener usually expresses agreement and support, whereas men point out the other side of the issue. Women see this as disloyalty and a refusal to offer support to their ideas. Women prefer other points of view expressed as suggestions and inquiries, rather than as direct challenges or arguments. Men are more comfortable with an oppositional style.

Men expect silent attention and interpret constant listener noise as signs of impatience on the listeners' part. When men don't make listening noises, women may assume they're not listening to them. Women make more listening noises such as "uh-huh ..." to encourage the other person. Men often believe these noises mean the woman agrees with him, when she may not agree with him at all. Because men don't make as many listening noises, women assume they're not really listening. Men are also less likely to make non-verbal signs of listening, and many continue doing whatever they were doing before the conversation began. Women are more likely to nod their head more, give direct eye contact, and stop whatever else they may have been doing when the conversation began.

Women often overlap and finish each other's sentences (normally, neither is offended). Men clam up or react defensively when women do this to them, because they feel the woman's trying to take over the conversation. Men feel it's rude to finish another's comments and shows lack of attention to what they're saying, but are more likely to interrupt with negative side comments.

FEEDBACK

Feedback is useful in both positive and negative contexts. Examples of positive feedback might include giving recognition for a job well done, or paying someone a sincere compliment. We'll be concentrating on the uses of feedback in dealing with negative or difficult situations.

Use feedback if you've been upset or annoyed by something someone has done. You identify what they're doing that bothers you and give them the opportunity to do something about it. We're being unfair to others when we don't communicate these issues to them.

Consider the following series of events:

- When a person does something that bothers you, a small blip occurs on your "screen of annoyance." Because it's only a small blip you decide to say nothing.
- The person does something else that annoys you, and another, bigger blip occurs on your "screen of annoyance."
- The blips soon accumulate, and you have a major blow-up with the person. The most trivial final incident can trigger this response.

How much better it would have been to handle each blip immediately and keep it from being recorded on your "screen of annoyance."

There are many different times when it is appropriate to use feedback. For example, you should:

- Let others know when you don't understand what they've said.
- Let others know when you like something they've said or done.
- Let others know when you disagree with them.
- Let others know when you think they've changed the subject or are going around in circles.
- Let others know when you're becoming annoyed.
- Let others know when you feel hurt or embarrassed.

Feedback also helps you keep in touch with your reactions, so you can deal with them before they turn into serious negative feelings of frustration, anger, hurt, defensiveness, defeat, fear, depression, dependence, weakness or defenselessness. Most women are comfortable saying that they have such feelings, but men have been socialized to believe it's a weakness to acknowledge them. This limits their options for expressing their feelings. Many respond as if they're angry—an acceptable reaction among men—when in reality they may feel hurt, or defenseless or afraid. Their ambiguous behavior confuses women and widens the communication gap between men and women. When men appear upset, often a woman will ask, "What's wrong?" The man's response is often "Nothing" or "I don't want to talk about it." This makes women feel "shut out" or rejected. This communication gap will be reduced if men stop and analyze what they're really feeling before they react.

Be selective when you use feedback. Ask yourself, "Am I about to unload this beef properly? Is my reaction unfair or petty?" Feedback must be immediate and specific—don't save up grievances and don't dump too many things on a person at once. As well, there must be something the recipient of the feedback can do about the problem.

To be effective, there must also be a foundation of trust between the sender and the receiver of the feedback. Otherwise, the feedback could be misinterpreted as a personal attack. The recipient may hear only critical things and react defensively rather than listen to what you have to say.

Here are some general guidelines for giving feedback:

1. *Be sure the receiver is ready.* Give the feedback only when there are clear indications that the receiver is ready to listen to it. If not, the receiver won't hear it or is likely to misinterpret your comments.
2. Base your comments on facts, not emotions. Giving feedback acts like a "candid camera." It's a report of the facts, rather than your ideas about why things happened or what the person meant by them.
3. *Be specific.* Give quotes and examples of exactly what you're referring to.
4. *Give feedback as soon after the event as possible*—the closer to the time the event took place, the better. If you give feedback

immediately, the receiver is more likely to understand exactly what's meant. The feelings accompanying the event still exist, so this, too, can help.

5. *Pick a convenient time.* Feedback is given when there's a good chance the person will listen to it. It may not be helpful if the receiver feels there are already other matters that demand his or her attention.

6. *Pick a private place.* Critical feedback given in front of others will be damaging rather than helpful.

7. *Concentrate on what can be changed.* Feedback should be about things that can be changed should the receiver choose to do so.

8. *Request cooperation.* The receiver can consider whether he or she wishes to attempt a change on the basis of your feedback information. You may wish to include that you would like to see certain changes. You're not likely to be successful if you give the impression of saying, "I've told you what's wrong with you, now change!"

9. *Focus on one thing at a time.* When learning how to give feedback, we may sometimes overdo it. It's as though we were telling the receiver, "I just happen to have a list of reactions here. Let me read them off to you." The receiver would naturally prefer time to consider each item and may balk at your overwhelming expectations.

10. *Be helpful.* Always consider your own motives for giving your opinions. Are you trying to be helpful to the receiver or are you unloading some of your own feelings? Are you using the occasion to try to get the receiver to do something that benefits only you? For example, if you're angry and wish to express it, say so—but include a description of the behavior that caused your anger.

11. *Encourage the recipient to provide feedback in return.* Giving feedback can become "one-upmanship." Because the giver has focused on the person's potential for improvement, the receiver goes away feeling as though he or she is "not as good." The exchange will be better balanced if the receiver has a chance to include some of his or her own feelings and concerns.

Here are some guidelines for receiving feedback:

1. *State what you want feedback about.* Help the giver provide useful reactions by asking for feedback about specific things.

2. *Check what you've heard.* Use paraphrasing to be sure you understand the giver's message.

3. *Share your reactions to the feedback.* As your own feelings become involved, you may forget to share your reactions to the feedback you've received. Knowing what was and was not helpful assists the giver to improve his or her ability to provide useful feedback. If the giver is uncertain about your reactions, he or she may be less apt to risk sharing in the future.

Here is an example of how to use feedback:

A receptionist had a problem she didn't know how to handle. She would take messages for all the office staff. One particular client (Mr. Samuels) phoned in repeatedly, asking to speak to Mr. Jacobs. She promptly passed on his messages. The fourth time he called, Mr. Samuels accused her of not passing on his messages to Mr. Jacobs. She wondered how she should deal with this situation as it was likely to happen again. What would you suggest she tell Mr. Samuels the next time he phoned?

Did you notice that she was trying to deal with the wrong problem? Her supervisor, Mr. Jacobs, was the problem, not Mr. Samuels. When I asked her if she had ever considered talking to her supervisor about the problem, she replied, "Oh, I couldn't do that!"

I then asked, "How is the situation going to change unless he knows what his behavior does to you? You're not even giving him the opportunity of solving this dilemma."

There are three steps in the process of feedback.

1. Describe the problem or situation to the person causing the difficulty.
2. Define what feelings or reactions (anger, sadness, anxiety, hurt or upset) the problem behavior causes you.
3. Suggest a solution or ask the person to provide a solution.

In the receptionist's case, she might have felt like saying, "You turkey, you never return your telephone messages!" But this kind of accusation would only get her supervisor's back up. Instead, she should try to gain his cooperation in solving the problem. She should say, "I have a problem and I need your help in solving it. Mr. Samuels phoned in four times, and he's really annoyed at me because you haven't returned his calls. This upsets me. What do you suggest I tell him the next time he calls?"

In this transaction, the following feedback steps were taken:

1. The problem—he's not returning his calls.
2. Her feelings or reactions—this upsets me.
3. The solution—she asks Mr. Jacobs to provide one.

Here's another example:

Margo, a co-worker, is always interrupting you with small talk, which interferes with your concentration. You're getting annoyed with her. Your first reaction might be to blast her with a statement such as, "Margo, will you shut up and let me get my work done!" Use feedback instead and say, "Margo, I'm working on an important project. I'm sure you're not aware of this, but every time you interrupt me, I lose my train of thought. Can we talk later at coffee break?"

1. The problem—she's interrupting your work.
2. Your feelings or reactions—you lose your train of thought.
3. The solution—you suggest talking later at coffee break.

Suppose Margo interrupts you again two hours later. What should you tell her? (Remember, this might be a habit with Margo, and she may have done it without thinking.) Your response? Repeat your original comments. "As I mentioned earlier, I'm working on an important project. Every time you interrupt me, I lose my train of thought. Can we talk later at coffee break?"

The next morning, guess what? She's at it again. What should you do now? Many would suggest that you ignore her comments. Instead say, "Margo, twice yesterday I mentioned that I'm working on an important project and your interruptions affected my concentration. Can you tell me why you're still doing this?"

What you're doing is making Margo account for her aggressive actions. (Yes, she's being aggressive, because she now *knows* she's bothering you.) Explain that if it happens again, you'll have to speak to

Jim, your supervisor. This is the step most people miss. It explains clearly the consequences Margo will face if she does it again. Margo promises she won't do it again.

Another day goes by, and Margo's at it again! What should you do the fourth time? Don't just say you're going to do something—follow through and talk to your supervisor.

Rather than giving the impression that you're going to "tattle" on your co-worker, ask for your supervisor's advice. Say, "Jim, I have a problem and I need your help in solving it. On Tuesday, I spoke to Margo and asked her to . . ." Explain everything you've done up to this point to stop her negative behavior. Then ask, "What do you suggest I do next time she interrupts me?"

Normally, he will talk to Margo himself, because Margo is wasting his department's budget and, ultimately, company money. As Margo reports to Jim, he is ultimately responsible for what she does—and she's making him look bad.

You might ask yourself, "Will Margo like me after I've spoken to my supervisor?" Who cares? She's going to cause you trouble whether you go to your supervisor or not.

Use the wording "I have a problem and I need your help in solving it" whenever someone is causing you grief. This is especially effective if used on the person who is causing the problem! You're not shaking your finger at them and bawling them out for their behavior. You're asking their help in trying to solve it.

This approach often gets the results you're after when other approaches fail. Use this feedback technique whenever a person's pen-clicking, gum-chewing, chair-squeaking or loud voice affects your performance at work. Use it when people are late with their reports, or when their actions keep you from doing your job correctly.

To recap the four major steps in the process of feedback:

1. Follow the three steps from the process of feedback.
2. Repeat step 1.
3. Ask the person to explain why he or she is continuing the annoying behavior. Explain the consequences should the behavior or situation happen again.

4. Follow through with the consequences.

Go directly to step 3 if faced with a person who refuses to cooperate.

Using Feedback with Very Difficult People

Among the wide range of human types, there are always a few people who are more difficult to deal with than others. A very difficult person isn't just someone who is having a bad day or with whom you have a personality conflict. A very difficult person is difficult often and with most people.

You *can* use feedback effectively for dealing with such people. However, because the risks are greater that your attempt will backfire, you need to prepare extra carefully before you approach them.

Thorough advance preparation is especially valuable when you're having problems with those in a position of power, such as your supervisor, a parent or an older person.

1. *Determine the problem.* Identify the specific behavior that's unacceptable; who is affected by the behavior; and how frequently it occurs. Concentrate on behavior the person can do something about. If the problem occurs only with one person, it's most likely a personality conflict rather than difficult behavior.
2. *Examine relationships.* Clues to the possible causes of the negative behavior will be found by examining how the difficult person interacts with others. Determining why the behavior occurs and why it's annoying you will help find solutions.
3. *Determine the cost of the problem behavior.* Whether it's lost productivity, general discomfort or lower morale, difficult behavior always carries a cost. The behavior should be ignored if you can't determine any costs.
4. *Prepare for the confrontation.* Should you have determined that the costs are too high, it's now time to speak to the offender. What special concerns do you have about the problem? What difficulties might you experience in the discussion? How will you handle these problems? Be ready for most situations you may face. Determine what you want to accomplish, then set up a meeting where you'll have privacy and enough time to discuss the situation.

5. *Rehearse thoroughly.* Rehearse the trying situation beforehand with a friend. Your friend should have as much knowledge of the situation as possible. This way, he or she can formulate good arguments and be able to anticipate what the other person's objections or reactions might be. The adage that practice makes perfect works here. Remember that the person you're eventually going to deal with has not had the opportunity to practice.

6. *Find a solution.* In a non-accusatory manner, explain why it concerns you. Give specific facts. Try not to offer your opinion as to why the problem exists. Ask questions to check your understanding. Identify the change in behavior you're seeking. Be open to changing your solution, if it's inappropriate. Listen to the person's ideas about how he or she can solve the problem. Express confidence in the person's ability to change.

7. *Agree on a plan of action.* Work towards a solution acceptable to both parties.

8. *Obtain a commitment.* Get agreement on specific actions the person will take, and set a deadline for these actions. Ask the person to confirm that he or she will do what's been agreed upon.

9. *Follow up with the person.* Recognize and comment on any progress you've observed. Re-evaluate the action plan and revise it if necessary. If there's been no change, repeat the process.

Coping Strategy

One solution may be to make the best of a bad situation. You can minimize the damage caused by the difficult behavior by:

- Remaining calm—Don't argue with the other person or make accusations.
- Using your listening skills to check your understanding.
- Being firm—Decide in advance what behavior you will or will not accept, and don't let yourself be pushed beyond this limit.
- Being persistent and consistent in your response, which conveys to the difficult person that you mean what you say.
- Believing in yourself and your ability to deal with others.
- Looking for ways to lessen your exposure to the behavior, or to reduce the causes of the behavior.

LISTENING

We spend up to 80 percent of our conscious hours using four basic communication skills: writing, reading, speaking and listening. Listening accounts for more than 50 percent of that time, so we're actually spending 40 percent of our waking time just listening!

We listen in spurts. Most of us are unable to give close attention to what's being said for more than sixty seconds at a time. We concentrate for a while, our attention lags, then we concentrate again.

Have you ever received specific training on how to listen? Probably not. It was always "Mary, will you stop talking ..." not "Mary, will you please listen."

How fast do you think the average person speaks in words per minute? (Keep in mind that secretaries usually take shorthand at 80 to 120 w.p.m., and court stenographers at about 220 w.p.m.)

Normal speaking speed is 125 to 150 w.p.m. My speaking speed is at least 160 w.p.m., even when I'm conducting seminars. This bothered me at one time.

Ask yourself what speed of speech you're capable of listening to. I've heard guesstimates of from 50 to 300 w.p.m. In reality, we're capable of listening at the phenomenal speed of 750 to 1,200 w.p.m.!

Then why don't we hear what people tell us? Because we're bored—that's why. There's not enough to keep our brain occupied when people speak at normal speeds. Even my speaking speed of 160 w.p.m. can't keep participants motivated during a seminar all the time. So what happens? We all go on side-trips where we may:

- start finding examples of something the person's discussing;
- wonder why our spouse was in such a bad mood that morning;
- admire something someone is wearing and wonder where they bought it;
- wonder if it's time for coffee break.

Radio and television have turned most of us into lazy listeners. For instance, did you turn the radio on this morning to catch the weather forecast or the news? Did you hear it? Or did you tune out the voices and miss it entirely? It takes practice and concentration to stay "tuned in" to what's being said.

There are several "problem listeners" that we all have to deal with. Here are a few.

Kinds of Bad Listeners

- *Bashful people.* Because shy people expect others to draw them out, they place emotional demands on everyone they're with. If they don't receive this attention, they tune out. Most shy people aren't aware of this negative behavior, nor of the demands it places on others around them.
- *Anxious people.* Because they lack confidence, they are nervous chatterers. They worry about what *they're* going to say next, which leaves little room for listening to others.
- *Argumentative people.* They'd argue with Einstein about his theory of relativity! They nitpick small details, which breaks conversational flow.
- *Opinionated people.* They spend their energy formulating arguments, rather than listening to others. They interrupt and begin every other sentence with "but . . ." These people may be overly anxious to impress others, but they often produce the opposite effect. People "tune them out."
- *Closed-minded people.* The most infuriating of bad listeners: they have rigid sets of values and find security in their prejudices. Any new ideas or changes leave them feeling threatened.

When faced with these poor listeners, use feedback to explain how you feel. Use of tact and empathy will assist you in helping them to become better listeners. Explain to closed-minded people that they've literally shut you out, that their unwillingness to listen to your ideas makes you feel rejected and unimportant. If you explain this and the person continues to behave the same way, you can (a) put up with it, or (b) use steps 2 to 4 of *Feedback Steps*.

Most poor listeners aren't aware of their failing. Your feedback may be helpful in changing their attitude and behavior.

Blocks to Effective Listening

There are other things that can lead you astray when listening. Ask yourself which ones are problems for you:

- You had trouble understanding the speaker's words or lacked the knowledge to grasp the message. (The speaker was using unfamiliar language, jargon or technical terms.)
- You were thinking of what you were going to say while the speaker was talking.
- You were preoccupied with how strongly you disagreed with the speaker's views.
- You listened for what you wanted to hear.
- You were too tired mentally to work at paying attention.
- There were outside noises and distractions.
- The speaker had poor delivery—slow, windy, irrelevant, rambling or repetitious.
- Something the speaker said intrigued you; you thought about it, and when you tuned back in you'd lost the thread.
- The speaker had an accent that you found difficult to understand.
- You tuned out because you thought you knew what the speaker's conclusions were going to be.
- You forgot to use paraphrasing and feedback in listening effectively.
- You felt you were being given far too much information.

How Do You Rate as a Listener?

Rate yourself (or have a friend help you) using the following scale:

Always = 5   Almost always = 4   Sometimes = 3
Rarely = 2   Never = 1

1. I allow the speaker to express his or her complete thoughts without interrupting.   _____
2. I actively try to develop my ability to remember important facts.   _____

3. In a conference or important phone conversation, I write down the most important details of a message. _____

4. I avoid becoming hostile or excited if a speaker's views differ from mine. _____

5. I repeat the essential details of a conversation back to the speaker to confirm that I have understood correctly. _____

6. I exercise tact in keeping the speaker on track. _____

7. I tune out distractions when listening. _____

8. I make an effort to show interest in the other person's conversation. _____

9. I understand that I'm learning little when I'm talking. (I talk too much, listen too little?) _____

10. I sound as if I'm listening. (I use paraphrasing, ask questions.) _____

11. I remember that people are less defensive when they feel they're being understood. _____

12. I understand that I don't have to agree with the speaker. _____

13. In personal conversation, I look for non-verbal forms of communication, such as body language, tone of voice and other signals that provide information in addition to the speaker's words. _____

14. I look as if I'm listening in personal meetings. (I lean forward, give eye contact.) _____

15. I ask for the spelling of names and places when I'm taking a message. _____

Scoring:

64 or more	You're an excellent listener!
50-63	You're better than average.
40-49	You require improvement!
39 or less	You're not an effective listener. You need practice, practice and more practice!

To elaborate on question 12: Suppose, in a conversation with someone about a controversial topic (such as abortion or capital punishment) you discover the two of you are on opposite sides of the issue. If your discussion is going nowhere but is making both of you angry, say: "You're entitled to your opinion, and I'm entitled to my opinion. Let's agree to disagree, and not discuss it any more."

To elaborate on question 15: When you're taking down people's names, ask them to confirm the spelling (even the name Smith may be spelled Smythe). In brackets (below the spelling of the name) add your own phonetic pronunciation of the name. For instance, the last name TOZER would be phonetically *Toezer*; BLECHA–*Blek-ka*; CARPHIN–*Car-fin*; CEBULIAK–*Ceb-u-lack*. This technique is very helpful to the person who will be returning the call. I use it on client files, so that I pronounce the person's name properly when I contact him or her in the future.

How to Improve Your Listening Skills

1. You must care enough to want to improve. Without this motivation, it'll be too much effort.
2. Try to find an uninterrupted area in which to converse. Keeping your train of thought is difficult when there are obstructions to concentration.
3. Try not to anticipate what the other person will say.
4. Be mindful of your own biases and prejudices, so they don't unduly influence your listening.
5. Pay careful attention to what's being said. Don't stop listening in order to plan a rebuttal to a particular point.
6. Be aware of "red flag" words that might trigger an overreaction or a stereotyped reaction. Examples of this are "women's libber" or "male chauvinist."
7. Don't allow yourself to get too far ahead of the speaker by trying to understand things too soon.
8. At intervals, try to paraphrase what people have been saying. Give them the opportunity to learn what you think you've heard them say.
9. When you have difficulty determining the point of the speaker's remarks, say, "Why are you telling me this?"
10. Watch for key or buzz words if you find you've lost the train of the conversation. This happens particularly when the speaker is long-winded or has a tendency to ramble.
11. Don't interrupt to demand clarification of insignificant or irrelevant details.

Qualities of a Good Listener

People who practice good listening skills do the following:

1. Let others finish what they're saying without interrupting them.
2. Ask questions if they're confused.
3. Pay attention to what others are saying and show they're paying attention by keeping comfortable eye contact. They don't let their eyes wander around the room.
4. Remain open-minded, ready to revise their opinion.
5. Use feedback and paraphrasing skills.
6. Pay attention to non-verbal signals such as the speaker's body language.
7. Don't "tune out" inappropriately when others are speaking.

SPEAKING

Another communication skill is the art of being able to say what you want to say. Verbal fluency enables you to express your thoughts clearly so others understand exactly what you mean. Here is a test you can give yourself. As we often don't see ourselves clearly, it might be a benefit to have a friend do it for you as well.

How Do You Rate as a Speaker?

Rate yourself using the following scale:

Always = 5   Almost always = 4   Sometimes = 3
Rarely = 2   Never = 1

1. If I were a listener, I would listen to myself.   _____
2. If I'm being misunderstood, I remember that it's my
   responsibility to help the other person understand me.   _____

3. I keep my instructions to others short, sweet and to the point. _____
4. I am aware of when my audience has tuned me out. _____
5. I make sure my listeners know what I want from them. _____
6. When I give instructions, I ask for feedback and paraphrasing
   to make sure I'm understood. _____
7. I make sure my non-verbal signals (body language,
   tone of voice, etc.) are the same as my verbal ones. _____
8. I make sure I don't intimidate my listeners with a loud voice,
   threatening appearance, intense or prolonged eye contact,
   verbal attacks, etc. _____
9. I articulate clearly. _____
10. I try to use language the listener can understand. _____

Scoring:

40 or more	You're an excellent speaker!
32-39	You're better than average.
25-31	You require improvement!
24 or less	You're not an effective speaker. You need practice, practice and more practice!

Did you chuckle to yourself when responding to the first statement? Did you find there was an element of truth in it? It's possible that you are one of those people who believe they're not worth listening to. There are three main reasons why you may feel you're not a good speaker.

1. *You have trouble getting the words out.* Some people know what they want to say, but can't quite say it. (They lack verbal fluency.) You could try joining Toastmaster or Toastmistress clubs or take a public-speaking course. Because you're going to be talking the rest of your life, it certainly seems worthwhile to improve this essential communication skill.
2. *You're not up on what's going on.* Often people insulate themselves from anything outside their own little world. Then, in social situations, they find they're not up on current events and have nothing to contribute to the conversation. The solution is to catch up on what's happening.
3. *You're a "motor-mouth."* Some people have problems keeping conversations short, sweet and to the point. Take the time to organize

your thoughts before you speak. Practice by writing down your thoughts, or use a tape recorder. Then reword your remarks, using more precise language.

The suggestions in point (3) will also be useful if you have trouble giving clear instructions. Use the KISS principle: Keep It Simple, Sweetie (or Keep It Simple, Stupid—depending on how you feel at the time).

To ensure that your listeners know what you want from them, ask them for their help before you give them the background information. For example:

A man wanted to discuss a work problem with his wife, who had just put in a rather tiring day herself. He proceeded to give her all kinds of details about what was happening. When he asked, "What do you think I should do?" she was embarrassed because she had been only half-listening. He had to tell her all the details again before she could answer. How much better it would have been, if he had started out the conversation, "Mary, I need your opinion on something that's happening at the office. Do you have time to discuss it right now?" Then he would have confirmed that she did have time, and she would have been aware that he needed her undivided attention.

Understanding Non-verbal Signals

You notice that the friend you're having lunch with has some food on the corner of her mouth. You want to bring this to her attention in a tactful way. You take your napkin and wipe your own face, but at the same time look at your friend's face where the food is. In many cases she will wipe her face too, though she wouldn't be able to explain why she did so.

We "hear" what people say partly through what their body language, tone of voice, etc., tell us. Being able to interpret non-verbal signals is probably one of the best assets anyone can have. If you want to be a good communicator, it's essential to be aware of and try to understand such non-verbal signals. The only people who can lie consistently without having their body language give them away are con artists and compulsive liars. This is because they actually believe the lies they're telling. Here are some examples of what body language can tell us:

- *Tapping fingers.* The person is annoyed, impatient or anxious.
- *Shifting weight from one foot to another.* The person has been standing too long, or is impatient.
- *Frowning.* The person doesn't understand what's being said or disagrees with what's being said.
- *Flushed face.* The person is embarrassed, angry or hot, or has high blood pressure. You'd have to look for other non-verbal signs to confirm which one it was.
- *Clenched jaw.* The person is upset, angry or anxious. This signal is more common in men than women.
- *Hand cupped around ear.* The person didn't hear what you said.
- *Slumped posture.* The person is tired, relaxed or depressed.
- *Avoidance of eye contact.* The person is shy, or bored. Or the person is from a culture that regards eye contact with the elderly or those in positions of authority as disrespectful. This signal is often misinterpreted as a sign of shifty behavior or a lack of self-confidence, when the cause may be something quite different.
- *Rapid or abrupt speech.* The person is upset, worried, anxious or angry.
- *Rise in voice volume.* The person is nervous or angry.
- *Rise in voice pitch.* A sign in women that the person is nervous or angry.
- *Drop in voice pitch.* A sign in men that the person is nervous or angry.
- *Jumpy body movements.* The person is nervous, anxious or angry.
- *Nose scratching.* The person is puzzled or dislikes something. Or the person's nose may be itchy.
- *Shrugging.* The person is indifferent or doesn't know the answer.
- *Forehead slapping.* The person feels forgetful or stupid.
- *Arms across chest.* The person feels defensive, physically cold or physically awkward. This may frequently be seen when men sit in chairs without arms.
- *Back slapping.* The person is offering congratulations, or perhaps encouragement.
- *Thumb and forefinger circling.* The person is saying "Okay," or "Right!" In some cultures this is seen as an obscene gesture.
- *Holding the hand up, palm outwards.* This means "Stop!"

- *Clasping both hands over head.* The person feels triumphant, pleased, successful.
- *Poking you in the ribs.* The person is sharing a joke or teasing you.

We often place our hand on the arm or shoulder of an upset person. With close friends, relatives, children or elderly persons, we might put an arm around their shoulder or hug them to give comfort.

We shake hands with people, an important non-verbal exchange. Originally, this communication meant that we were extending our empty weapon hand to show that we came as a friend. Now it can mean that we are giving our word that the exchange to follow is above board; that we are trustworthy. Women in business should practice until they feel comfortable giving a firm handshake. At a job interview, candidates should offer their hand first, rather than wait for the interviewer to do so. This indicates a high degree of self-confidence in a way that's hard to duplicate.

When you're interested in what others are saying, you might lean forward. You might also lean forward when you wish to speak next.

When people feel they are in a position of power, they often show dominance by deliberately interrupting others. They stand with feet straddled, hands on hips (a parental stance). They may fail to step aside when on a collision course with others. They may hold eye contact longer than is comfortable for the recipient, or hover or lean over others while watching them work. (If someone does this to you, stop working and use the feedback technique to explain what their behavior is doing to you.)

Men who want to show their power will straddle a chair. Others will put their feet up on a desk and ostentatiously not remove them when someone comes into the room.

Power-hungry people take up more space on couches or benches than is their due. Don't encourage people to do this at the expense of others. Do something!

I remember one time when I had been traveling all day and was bone tired. There was a one-hour wait between connections at an airport. The place was crowded with travelers. I spotted a man sitting at one end of a bench. Taking up the rest of the bench were his briefcase, suitcase and overcoat.

I approached him and asked, "Is this your briefcase?" He nodded. I removed the briefcase from the bench and placed it in front of him.

"Is this your suitcase?" He nodded. I removed the suitcase from the bench and placed it in front of him.

Before I could ask him, "Is this your overcoat?" he removed it and placed it on his lap. I smiled and sat down right next to him.

Shortly after, two other tired travelers joined us on the bench. Their body language and smiles thanked me for the effort I had made.

People who lack assurance show this by their body language as well. Their posture shows defeat, there's little eye contact, their voices are soft. They take up as little space as possible (pull all their "ends" in) or wear a fixed smile.

People who are lying may give themselves away through non-verbal signals. When people are being open with you, their body language usually indicates openness. They show their hands openly, for example. When they are hiding something, their body language changes. They may hide their hands in their pockets or behind their backs. If you accuse them of something, they'll likely give you an incredulous look and reply, "Who me?" They may put their hand on their chest (a non-verbal sign of honesty. NOTE: The hand-to-the-chest gesture when used by women may also be a protective gesture showing sudden surprise or shock), but other body language may contradict this. Look for signals such as:

- avoiding eye contact (usually by looking down)
- blinking rapidly
- twitching and swallowing repeatedly
- clearing the throat and wetting the lips often
- covering the mouth when speaking
- shrugging
- rubbing the nose
- scratching the head while talking
- putting a hand on the throat
- rubbing the back of the neck

Space Bubbles

We all have a "space bubble" around us—a gap between us and others that we need to maintain to feel secure. For most people, this bubble extends eighteen to twenty-four inches from their bodies.

There are several types of distances we normally keep between ourselves and others. These are:

- *Intimate distance.* Only people we trust are welcome within our "space bubble." We welcome people who are near and dear to us into this space, but we often have to endure others as well. This can be at the theatre, on a bus, at a seminar or in an elevator. You can probably think of hundreds of instances where we have to tolerate this closeness.

    Watch yourself when you're in an elevator. You naturally pull in all your *ends* and take up as little space as possible. Should you inadvertently touch the stranger next to you, you'll automatically say, "Oops, I'm sorry," and pull away. This would also happen if you touched someone in a bank lineup, or at a checkout counter.
- *Personal distance* is the space you usually keep with others when you have enough room to be comfortable. This is anywhere between three and four feet, depending on your comfort zone and how well you know the person. In elevators, as soon as the crowd thins, people will automatically widen the space between themselves and others.
- *Social distance* is four to seven feet. Strangers or acquaintances sitting on chairs or couches at a party will try to maintain this distance.
- *Far social distance.* This could happen at a large party or be the distance between a speaker and his or her audience.
- *Territorial supremacy.* Not only do we try to keep a certain quantity of space around us, but also we try to retain physical control over anything we think belongs to us. This may be a desk at work; our bedroom, kitchen or workshop; our car or boat; or our brush and comb. Others may use these articles only when we've given them permission to do so. That is why we may react violently when someone takes something of ours without permission.

The office receptionist is often the victim of "territorial invasions." Other office workers somehow think that it's okay to help themselves to the Post-it notes or the stapler on her desk. They may even open her desk drawers and help themselves to her scissors or ruler. Try to remember that that desk is *hers*. Don't take anything that you haven't asked permission to use. Should you be the receptionist, designate a communal area where such equipment can be kept. For example, keep an extra pad of Post-its, a ruler, a stapler and a pair of scissors on top of a filing cabinet. Make others aware that equipment in this area is theirs, while your desk is *yours*.

People have the psychological upper hand when they're in their own territory. Salespeople are very aware of this. If the client comes to the seller's place of business, the seller has the advantage. If the salesperson goes to the potential client's place of business, the client has the advantage. That is why salespeople often try to find a neutral ground on which to sell their products.

This psychological truth also holds when a supervisor has to discipline an employee. If the situation isn't serious, the supervisor will likely go to the employee's territory, so that the employee will feel less threatened, or will arrange to discuss the matter on neutral territory, such as an empty office or a cafeteria. Privacy is a must in all cases.

With a more serious problem, the supervisor will most likely have the employee come to his or her office, where he or she will have more power and the employee will feel less secure. There are degrees of intimidation here, too. For the employee, the least threatening environment in the supervisor's office is at a round table of some sort. Next is beside the supervisor's desk. In the most threatening arrangement the supervisor is behind the desk with the subordinate sitting opposite. To increase the quelling effect the supervisor might arrange for the subordinate to sit in a lower chair than the supervisor. Or a supervisor who is small in stature might stand up to give a more powerful impression.

Eye Contact

Variations in eye contact convey a great deal. Comfortable eye contact is three seconds. If you hold eye contact longer than three seconds, you are invading another's body space as directly as if you had touched him or her. Many aggressive people use a fixed stare to intimidate others. They could be one hundred feet away from you, but you'd still feel their invasion of your space.

You may have used extended eye contact yourself when you've been very angry with someone. You looked them right in the eye as you spoke to them. If a person says, "He was shooting darts at me," that person was probably giving full eye contact for too long, possibly reinforced by an angry expression.

Blinking eyes may indicate either lying or nervousness. Unblinking eyes with eye contact could mean the person is lying and watching for your reaction. Or the person could be intensely interested in what you're saying.

A wink can show either intimacy or lack of seriousness. The latter may be directed at parents when you're telling a "white lie" to their child.

Arguments

Should you have to referee an argument, I suggest you put your knowledge of body language to the test. The body language of bystanders observing the argument can tell you what the observers believe and whose side they're on. If they've had the opportunity of learning the facts of the case, they'll automatically take sides. When this happens, they'll copy the body language of the person they think is in the right. The more observers there are the better, because they'll unknowingly choose sides. You'll then have a running start refereeing the argument.

3

DEALING WITH MANIPULATORS

There are two kinds of manipulation—positive and negative. An example of positive manipulation is when you encourage others to do something, to give them the belief that they can do something they don't think they can do. However, many of these "games," as we define them, use negative manipulation. They use indirect and unclear communication. Often the person "playing the game" is not even aware that he or she is doing so. Here are 115 ways people manipulate others and methods used to deal with those behaviors.

PASSIVE MANIPULATORS

Passive people do not respect themselves, do not express their needs, nor defend their rights. Here are some of the ways they try to manipulate others:

FEAR VICTIMS

Fear victims allow fear to control their lives and are so ruled by anxiety, and the fear it arouses, that they avoid the situation and thus avoid assertiveness. For example: Agoraphobics. These people have panic attacks when they even attempt to leave their homes. A university study showed that, of the things people fear—40 percent never happen, 30 percent have happened, 22 percent are needless petty or small, 8 percent are real but divided into: those you can solve and those you cannot solve. To overcome:

1. *Have patience with them.*
2. *Have them identify the worst thing that could happen to them.*
3. *Have them identify what the chances are for the worst to happen.*
4. *If their fear is deeply routed, suggest that they receive counseling to overcome their fears.*

EVERYONE MUST LOVE ME

These people's goal is to have everyone—spouse, lover, children, boss, friends, shopkeepers and even the man who comes to the door selling magazines—think they're the greatest. They feel like failures if they don't please everybody (an impossible task). To overcome:

1. *Help them identify when others are using them.*
2. *Assist them to find ways to handle situations where others are using them.*
3. *Praise them when they stand up for themselves.*
4. *Constantly remind them that they can't please everybody all the time.*

SUPER AGREEABLES

They always smile and have a friendly word for you. People instantly like them. They promise that whatever you want from them you'll get. However, they let you down and don't deliver what they promise. They're very attentive to you as a person, but do not pay close attention to what you're saying—they simply nod as if they agree. To overcome:

1. *Let them know you're counting on them to do what they've promised to do.*
2. *Praise them for good work.*

HEAD-BURIERS

When their fight-or-flight response kicks in, they simply freeze. They don't fight or run away, but become immobilized—unable to think or function. They abdicate or stay away from work when important decisions must be made, hoping that somebody else will handle it. These people are highly prone to stage fright, which can render them speechless. To overcome:

1. *Suggest they take an assertiveness training course.*
2. *Rehearse situations with them that make them freeze.*
3. *Give them deadlines for responses to situations that immobilize them now.*

BASHFUL

They're so shy that it's painful to watch them interact with others. The least little thing will cause them to blush beet red, perspire heavily, stammer their words, and readily show with their non-verbal communication that they're greatly embarrassed. They have nightmares about situations they will face the next day, and by the time the situation occurs, they've worked themselves up until they're almost immobilized. People react by being super-careful while they're around this kind of person, and some shun them altogether because of the guilt they feel when they inadvertently make the other person respond bashfully. These people are prone to a lot of teasing from stronger individuals, and suffer terribly. To overcome: follow the steps for "Head Buriers."

INDECISIVES

They have a terrible time making decisions, and ask everyone they meet for help in making them. They're noted for wavering between several choices or changing their course of action three or four times before making even a tentative decision. They seek the perfect solution, and are on edge if they can't find one. Once they make a decision, they discover a flaw in it and change their minds again. They're wishy-washy and inconsistent, swaying back and forth between choices. To overcome:

1. *When they come to you asking for direction, ask them, "What do you think you should do?" Eventually, they will see that they're capable of making decisions for themselves.*
2. *Ask yourself whether this person should be in a position that involves making decisions. Many people are more comfortable having others make decisions for them.*
3. *If they must make decisions, have them give several solutions, then encourage them to make a decision.*
4. *Give deadlines if decisions must be made.*

STALLERS

They bury their head in the sand hoping that, if they put off making a decision long enough, the problem will go away or someone else will make the choice for them. They're very consistent in their inability to make a decision, and they assume their choice won't be the right one. Even the simplest of errors will lower their sense of self-worth. They may use delaying tactics to get even with others. To overcome:

1. *Have them write down all their choices.*
2. *Give pros and cons for each choice.*
3. *Decide which choice is best.*
4. *Write steps they'll take to make it happen.*

SELF-BERATERS

They're always putting themselves down, and appear to need others to constantly give praise—whether it's earned or not. Everything that goes wrong must be their fault. They seek reassurance from others but defeat the effort by berating their own actions at every move. They're highly critical of their work and actions. Most are average performers, but they almost beg others to find fault with everything they do. To avoid being hurt by others, they identify their faults before anyone else can do it for them. To overcome:

1. *Encourage them to do assignments they do well.*
2. *Get them to talk about their concerns.*

3. *Explain the cost of begging for reassurance, how people lose faith in their ability.*

PUSHOVERS

These people can be coerced into doing almost anything that others want them to do. They have difficulty saying "No" to anyone because they feel guilty. To overcome:

1. *Pick one relationship or type of situation where they've said "yes" inappropriately several times during the past three or four months.*
2. *Determine their motivation for saying "yes." Were they concerned that "no" might injure the relationship? Are they worried about the other person's feelings?*
3. *Put together a plan of action for preventing this next time. Part of this step involves preparing themselves for the occasion—the other in preventing the occasion from recurring.*
4. *Practice their new response with someone who has good judgment and isn't involved in the situation.*

PASSIVE-RESISTANT MANIPULATORS

These are passive people who are trying to become more assertive in their behavior. They mutter and sigh a lot and play manipulative games to get their way. They haven't learned to ask up-front for what they want.

SUFFERERS

Sufferers get what they want by sending indirect messages, many through their body language. They may play the part of the martyr—act overworked, persecuted or totally dependant. They sigh a lot—and utter indirect complaints. They're trying to say, *"If you appreciated me, or even noticed all the things I do for you, you'd want to do more for me."* To overcome:

1. *Remember that you have a choice as to whether you do or do not accept the guilt they're trying to give to you.*
2. *Tell them what you think they're trying to do. "Your comments show me that you're trying to make me feel guilty about. . . . Is that true?"*
3. *If there is truth to their statements, try to rectify the situation.*
4. *Talk about what their body language is telling others.*

UNINVOLVED

The deliberately uninvolved person, is never wrong—but is never right either. These people may say they don't care which decision is made, but their body language shows otherwise. To overcome:

1. *Insist that they clearly state what they want.*
2. *If they won't state their opinion say, "So you don't care which movie we see?"*
3. *Explain how their non-verbal communication is differing from their words.*

"I WON'T FIGHT"

These people appear to agree, but don't support anyone else's ideas unless they happened to be the same as theirs. To overcome: Use same tactics as "Uninvolved."

SHAM ASSERTIVE

People in this category have problems in any but the most superficial relationship. They may seem open, assertive, warm and even extroverted, but this covers for a lack of honesty. This person would state, *"How wonderful to hear from you—I was just thinking about you."* (Completely untrue—you know the person detests you). To overcome:

1. *Say, "I know you're not my greatest fan, so I appreciate your efforts to be friendly."*
2. *If it's someone you associate with on a regular basis, be polite and courteous, but don't let your guard down.*

WHINERS, COMPLAINERS AND BELLYACHERS

They're chronic gripers who grumble about everything—publicly and privately. They're crybabies who voice protracted protests over the unimportant. Driven by childish insecurity, they complain when everything's actually going well. They love to exaggerate unfair workloads, tardy reports, broken rules—whatever they can blame on somebody else. Although their work is good, they usually don't sound off about legitimate problems. When whiners warn you of trouble ahead, their intent is to establish an excuse in advance of a feared failure. To overcome:

1. *When they start griping, obtain their permission to let you help them find solutions to their problems. If they don't allow you to help, go to step 7. If they accept your help, proceed to step 2.*
2. *Have them write down the SPECIFIC problem. (This might take some time to determine.)*
3. *Ask them to write down all the possible solutions to the problem. You can suggest others.*
4. *Have them identify the benefits/disadvantages (pros and cons) of each solution. Using a point system might help. For instance, possibly the cost of solving the problem might be crucial.*
5. *Have THEM choose the best solution. (They might say, "What do you think I should do?" Don't take the bait—because if you suggest a solution and it isn't effective, they'll be the first to say, "I told you it wouldn't work!")*
6. *Have them write the steps they will take to achieve the solution (giving deadlines).*
7. *Refuse to talk about the topic in the future. (An ideal tactic to use if you've become a whiner, complainer and bellyacher yourself or have to make complicated decisions).*

KILLJOYS

These people are negative thinkers who affect the morale of everyone around them. They're also whiners, complainers and bellyachers. They're experts at giving you reasons why it's wrong to enjoy life. These wet blankets intend to take the pleasure out of life for themselves and others. They berate those who seem to enjoy life and encourage others to take life "more seriously." It's hard for others to enjoy their work in such a rigid environment. To overcome:

1. *Use feedback to explain what their behavior is doing to those around them.*
2. *Encourage them to concentrate on what's good about life rather than what's bad.*
3. *Suggest they take an assertiveness training course to change their approach to life.*

BOOTLICKERS

They fawn over and do special favors for their bosses (that have nothing to do with work). They preen before they enter their boss's office—doing up their suit jackets, slicking their hair, correcting their posture. Some become the office tattle-tale. They're manipulative and want to get noticed by using the wrong means. To overcome: (If you're a boss)

1. *Take them aside and explain your aversion to this kind of behavior.*
2. *Watch that you don't show favoritism to this type of employee.*
3. *When they've done well, be sure to praise them, and encourage them to praise others.*

"YES MEN"

Insincerely give extravagant praise so they can use you. They believe if they constantly say things designed to please you (greatly exaggerating reality) you'll do as they ask. They're afraid their plan, procedure, policy or assignment can't stand on its own merit, so they use unwarranted praise to gain acceptance of them. To overcome: use same techniques as for "Bootlickers."

RENEGERS

They make promises they never intend to keep. They mislead you by breaking promises they hadn't planned to keep in the first place.

To overcome:

1. *Have them give an oral (in public if possible) or written commitment to you.*
2. *Make sure they know the consequences, should they let you down in the future.*

OVERCOMMITTERS

These are nice people who can't say "no" to others' requests. However, they often find they haven't time to do what they've promised. They love harmony and hate to argue, so they'll agree to do what others ask them to do. They avoid confrontation, not wanting to hurt others' feelings. They promise too much or say they'll do something they don't really want to do. Unable to handle it all, they put off action or making decisions and break their promises. They don't hurt others intentionally but often cause difficulty for those who are depending on them to follow through. To overcome:

1. *Have them make a commitment to you that they WILL do what they've promised to do.*
2. *When necessary, you make the decision.*
3. *If they do commit themselves, explain that you're counting on them.*

SHOWOFFS

They must be the center of attention. They accomplish this by escalating the value of what they do, where they've been, and who they know. They exaggerate their own importance to win admiration or attention and have the habit of snubbing people they don't think of as important. They're snooty and snobbishly superior. Being high achievers, they put themselves high on their list of priorities. To overcome:

1. *Watch that they don't take an unfair share of credit for assignments done with others.*
2. *Give them praise where praise is deserved, and correct them when they try to exaggerate their contributions.*
3. *Use feedback to explain what their behavior is doing to others.*

MAGNIFIERS

These people make mountains out of mole hills—everything is a disaster. They blow minor tasks out of proportion to make themselves appear more important. They can be "wet blankets" who are very negative, throwing cold water on every new idea. They enlarge whatever they do, making even the insignificant a very big deal. They're immature in their desire to impress others with unimportant work. They often complain that they haven't time for their important assignments. They're too busy attempting to get noticed by giving each little job all they've got, whether or not it deserves the effort. Most are perfectionists. To overcome:

1. *Help them choose priorities and the time expected to complete assignments.*
2. *Develop a color code for assignments which identifies deadlines (red is urgent, must be done right away; orange must be done today; green includes required date of completion).*

EVADERS

These people hate controversy, confrontation and arguing, so they remain silent. They're likeable people but keep their ideas to themselves, which protects them from others discounting their ideas. Even when they're upset or angry, they refuse to criticize. They feel that they're not in control in confrontational situations, so they don't say what they think. To overcome:

1. *Have them write down their ideas relating to an issue, then make an appointment for you to discuss the controversial issue. Explain that you expect them to be honest, and promise that you'll listen to their ideas.*
2. *At your meeting, get directly to the point—ask to see their prepared information. Don't let them leave your meeting until they've expressed their ideas or side of the discussion.*

GRINNERS

They keep quiet rather than state their disagreement. When aggravated, rather than show they're agitated, they respond with a grin that is more of a grimace. Their nervous gestures signal their true feelings, even though they may feel angry or hurt. They passively keep their feelings to themselves. No matter what happens, they grin. This ambiguous set of signals confuses others, who instinctively feel that something is wrong. To overcome:

1. *Use feedback to explain that you're aware of their displeasure.*
2. *Ask open-ended questions. "I can see that you don't agree and welcome your suggestions. How do you see us solving this problem?"*
3. *Wait for their reply. Don't let them shrug off their opinions.*

WORRIERS

They bottle up their negative feelings, seeing only the dark side of every issue. They're chronic worriers who expect the worst. They jump to conclusions and make assumptions rather than ask for clarification about the true situation. These worry-warts mull over the situation until they convince themselves that things will go wrong. Some worry to the state where they're stressed to their limit and can't cope at all. To overcome:

1. *Assume that withdrawal from them indicates unexpressed hurt.*
2. *Give constant feedback on their performance. Make sure they know exactly what you want from them.*
3. *These people need very detailed job descriptions, with standards of performance (identifying quality, quantity and time) that outline exactly what you want from them.*

MARTYRS

They complain how they've sacrificed for you, detail all they've done for you. They crave constant praise for their work. Many are workaholics, who complain about all they have to do yet won't ask anyone for help. By doing this, they hope that others will become dependent upon them and will show appreciation for their efforts. Their workaholism can mask problems in their personal or social lives. Whenever things go wrong, they're never at fault, so they're great at buck-passing. They complain about the amount of work they have, but their frantic pace sets a standard that others find almost impossible to meet. To overcome:

1. *Learn to say "no" when they volunteer to do too much.*
2. *Suggest they keep "To Do" lists.*
3. *Make sure they have up-to-date job descriptions with standards of performance, and make sure they do only their own assignments.*

PHONEY LLLNESSES

These people use illness (phoney or real) to get attention from others. Many learned this tactic as children, when their mothers gave them much more attention when they were sick. They crave attention, but for some reason they aren't obtaining the amount they require. Some even become hypochondriacs—thinking every ailment could be fatal. To overcome:

1. *Give them the attention they crave.*
2. *Keep them busy doing things they like to do and are good at.*

CHILDISH

They play games on others—interrupt them with childish antics. They can have the "class clown" mentality where they seek others' attention by fooling around. Getting them to accomplish tasks can be a heavy chore. To overcome:

1. *Arrange a meeting to discuss your displeasure.*
2. *Show your encouragement when they improve.*
3. *If they act up at meetings—take them aside.*
4. *A clearly defined job description that includes set standards of performance on how they are to complete tasks should help.*
5. *If behavior continues, begin disciplinary steps with written warnings.*

INDIRECT AGGRESSIVE MANIPULATORS

These people are between assertive and obviously aggressive in the behavior they exhibit. They use subtle, underhanded means to get their way, such as sabotage, sarcasm, the silent treatment and gossip.

SABOTEUR

These people express their objections to a request covertly—by resorting to sabotage. For example: the secretary who doesn't believe she should have to make coffee—so one time she uses half a package and the next a package and a half when making the coffee. To overcome:

1. *Obtain proof that they have indeed sabotaged.*
2. *Ask them why they did what they did.*
3. *Explain your expectations.*
4. *Tell them the consequences if something similar happens in the future.*
5. *If serious enough—and you have proof—document their behavior and initiate termination of the employee.*

SARCASTIC

These people resort to a type of sarcasm that is cruel and relies on put-down barbs that talk about your flaws. Find more information on this topic in Chapter 5.

SILENT TREATMENT

These people are unresponsive and refuse to tell you why they're silent. They silently express their anger through fixed, hostile looks while retreating into themselves. Sometimes their silence is intimidating because you don't know what it means, how to deal with it, or what you've done to warrant such behavior. This is also discussed in Chapter 5.

STICKY-IFFIES

They start by praising you and end up with a qualifying put-down. These left-handed complimenters catch you off guard the first time. You feel so good about the praise that you don't realize until later that it had a hidden negative implication tied to it. A little later, you wonder if you just imagined the slap—or if it was really intended. The two-sided remark was meant as a barb. Trying not to show signs of being stung, you feel yourself smile and hear yourself sputter thanks while knowing that's not the way you should respond. Then you kick yourself for having thanked somebody who just got away with putting you down.

Examples of this are:

"You can lift a lot of weight for someone so small."
"You're in great shape for a person your age."
"You're almost as smart as your sister."
"You make a lot of money for a woman."
"You're really agile for a person your size."

To overcome:

1. *Divide the remark into two parts—praise and put-down.*
2. *Reply to the person, "I don't know how you expect me to react to your last comment. On one hand, you've given me a compliment, then you've pulled the rug out from under me by giving me a put-down. Which way did you intend me to receive it?" (This informs the person that you're onto the game.)*

GOSSIP

These people are rumor mongers who spread unverified or expanded stories. Their intent is to gain attention for themselves by spreading untrue or partly true messages. They often embroider the story, filling in the blanks to make it appear more important or believable or how they think it "should" be. They forget details, remembering only vivid parts and distorting the facts by omitting vital information. To overcome:

1. *Cut short discussions that are obviously meaningless and spiteful gossip.*

2. *Ask a lot of questions. (They won't likely have answers or will "paint themselves into a corner" with their embellishments.)*
3. *Check the facts before reacting.*

SNITCHERS

Snitchers childishly tattle on their co-workers and spread gossip. This can be due to jealousy, to pay others back for some perceived wrong, or so they look better to their superiors. They try to discredit others. To overcome:

1. *Use feedback to explain your displeasure at their using this kind of behavior.*
2. *Make sure you praise them for their accomplishments.*
3. *Determine whether you've been encouraging this kind of behavior by your actions.*

SNIPERS

They hit you when you're not looking with barbed words and innuendos. Their attacks can be subtle or their sniping can be hidden behind sarcastic comments or cruel jokes. Their most damaging attacks can occur in public—perhaps at a meeting. They often act the "class clown" persona, and their unkind jabs could be mistaken for humor. Others may laugh, but most are not comfortable with the cruelty shown; they can sense that there could be a hidden agenda behind the sniper's words. Even if the victim retaliates, the sniper has accomplished his or her goal—that of degrading his or her enemy in public. To overcome:

1. *Confront the sniper—in private if possible, in public if necessary.*
2. *See information on how to deal with sarcasm, in Chapter 5.*
3. *Outline consequences should the behavior happen again—and be sure to follow through.*

ENVIOUS/JEALOUS

These people suffer from jealousy and resentment, and cannot accept that you've earned whatever recognition or status you've achieved in life. They feel that your achievements were obtained through "luck" and that they're deprived because life hasn't been so kind to them. To put you down (and make themselves feel more important) they try to discredit your accomplishments. They want revenge, and even if the attack is unprovoked, they may vent their frustration on you with hostile acts. To overcome:

1. *Use feedback to identify what you see them doing. Ask them to account for why they're acting the way they are. Then try to keep your future talks on a friendly level.*
2. *Encourage and give them praise for authentic acts.*
3. *Show an interest in them—their goals, ambitions and successes—but downplay their perceived failures.*

STEAL LIMELIGHT

You may do all the work, but they somehow find a way to take all the credit. They can be very devious and hard to detect or protect against. To overcome:

1. *Confront them in private and ask them to explain their actions. "This is the same issue I brought up at our last meeting. Why are you trying to give the impression that this is your idea?"*
2. *Don't discuss new ideas with them unless someone else knows ahead of time or it's in writing, possibly in a memo.*
3. *Bring up important issues they may take credit for, at meetings or in the company of credible witnesses.*

IMPOSTERS

They pretend they're something they're not—overemphasize everything they do as being bigger and better than everyone else. To overcome:

1. *Ask for facts to back up their claims.*

TWO-FACED

They "talk out of both sides of their mouths." They're hypocrites, who double-deal others with intentional misrepresentation or deception. To your face, they pretend to be your friend, but you may find out the hard way that they're not. They may deceive you into believing that the data they give you verbally for inclusion in your report is correct when in fact it's not. Therefore, your entire report is useless, making you (not them) look bad. To overcome:

1. *Ask questions requiring direct answers.*
2. *Have them send information in writing, so they can't dispute the information given.*
3. *Protect yourself in the future by checking every item to ensure that the information is indeed factual.*

AMBIGUOUS

They use forked tongues to intentionally send you ambiguous, contradictory messages. Dealing with them is extremely frustrating because they keep you off balance. They do not respond as people expect; therefore, many control the situation simply because others don't know what they're up to. By the time others figure it out, it's too late. To overcome:

1. *Let go of your anger. Then explain with feedback what their behaviour is doing to you and others. Try to keep your talk friendly and impersonal—not an attack.*
2. *Follow steps for "Two-faced."*

BLUFFERS

They pretend to have considerable knowledge when discussing issues, and are so convincing with their jargon that others believe their lies. Assumptions are passed on as facts. They give the impression that they've almost completed a task when in reality they haven't started it yet, because they're not sure what needs to be done and have doubts whether they can do the job. When they're in over their heads, they usually procrastinate. They're expert stallers, believing that if they wait long enough, someone else will do the work. To overcome:

1. *Make sure they know clearly what you want from them and when you want it, in writing if possible.*
2. *Check their progress on a regular basis.*
3. *Let them know you're counting on them to complete the assignment.*

CAMOUFLAGERS

They trade favors with others: *"I'll do this for you, if you do that for me."* However, they aren't honest about their side of the bargain. Because of their friendly attitude, you believe you've made an honest trade. However, they have hidden agendas, and are prone to giving half-truths or leaving out crucial details. They aren't honest with you, always hiding the real reason behind their requests. They constantly maneuver and manipulate. They're so busy trading favors, they're barely able to get anything done. You do as they ask, then find yourself disappointed and frustrated because they don't live up to their end of an agreement. To overcome:

1. *Get everything in writing, possibly through two-part memo forms that allow you to ask questions in the top portion and provide space for the answer in the bottom section. Then it's in writing and they can't deny their commitments.*
2. *Make them stick to the facts, showing the research behind their findings.*
3. *Don't trade favors with this kind of individual, unless you can get the agreement in writing.*
4. *If you're their boss, don't let them away with this kind of behavior. Follow up at regular intervals to ensure they're progressing as expected.*

GUILT-GIVERS

We live in a guilt-ridden society. Not only do we give guilt to ourselves, but we accept even unwarranted guilt from others. Some people are experts at guilt-giving and love wallowing in self-pity. A client wants you to break company rules for them and tries to make you feel guilty when you won't. Your parent whines, "If you loved me more, you'd come over to see me more often." Often they feel guilty about something they did but refuse to accept the responsibility, attempting to pass the guilt on to others instead. To overcome:

1. *Refuse to accept the guilt. Ask them, "Are you trying to make me feel guilty because . . . ?"*
2. *Recognize that this is their problem—not yours.*

ONE-UPPERS

They're similar to Showoffs but go at it more aggressively. No matter how much you know, they know more. They're pompous, pretentious, misleading, and can talk with such assurance that you're absolutely convinced they speak the truth. Many learn the hard way that they're completely inept. They repeat their own lies about their competency so often that they fool even themselves into believing they're the experts they pretend to be. They embellish the data they have and amplify it. To overcome:

1. *Press for facts and details relating to their allegations.*
2. *Have them put things in writing, so you have something concrete to question.*
3. *If they continue, use feedback to confront them with your findings.*

SKEPTICS

They're suspicious, and wary of trusting others. They've likely been let down many times by others, and so are very skeptical of the motives of new people. They research until they have every detail, then question others' knowledge of the topic. This makes them good detail-people, who can be an asset to a company, but it drives others to distraction. They analyze information to death, and are not content until they have every little detail. Dealing with them can be very irritating to the average person, who has neither the drive nor the time for such analysis of data. To overcome:

1. *Always have your data ready for them. If you're the one requesting the information, make sure to let them know exactly what you want from them—not reams of unnecessary information.*
2. *Give them assignments that will allow them to use their talents for analyzing and retrieving data.*
3. *Understand that it will take time to gain their trust.*

PASS-THE-BUCK

Problems are never their fault, but someone else's. They shift the blame to others for their own mistakes. They use expressions such as *"You always . . ."* or *"You never . . ."* If they think they might fail, they can become highly stressed. If they detect they might have a problem completing an assignment, they do everything they can to pass the problem assignment to others. They have trouble accepting blame and criticism, and so do their best to stay clear of situations where they might be blamed for a blunder. They're heard to say, *"I didn't know I was responsible for that!"* or *"You didn't tell me you needed that today!"* To overcome:

1. *When delegating assignments, make sure they know that they're responsible for the task and when you expect it to be completed.*
2. *Encourage them to ask for help if they run into difficulties. Help them find a solution—but don't accept the problem as being yours.*
3. *Encourage them to take responsibility for their own actions. Reassure them that it's all right to make a mistake—but not all right to blame others for their mistakes.*

AGGRESSIVE MANIPULATORS

Aggressive people have little respect for other people's needs and rights. Things go their way or not at all. They railroad, bulldoze, and shove their ideas and wishes on others, using persistence, coercion and even threats. They differ from other manipulators because they're obvious. You know they're out to get you.

HOSTILE

These habitually belligerent people take their anger out on you. They're so weighed down by jealousy, rage or resentment that only by throwing stones at others do they get the lift they need to go on. This causes others to defend themselves or retaliate. To overcome:

1. *Wait till they've calmed down. Don't let them bait you into making statements you don't want to make (the temptation to retaliate will be strong).*
2. *Talk about matters with them in a calm manner.*
3. *Agree on how you're going to proceed.*
4. *Encourage them to obtain help in handling their anger.*

BULLIES

Bullies use fear, cruelty and threats to control others. Although they often fool others into believing they have high self-esteem, the opposite is true. That's why they go after those who appear weak and passive. The hair on the back of your neck will rise when these people enter the room. Instead of behaving submissively around them, stand your ground. To overcome:

1. *Let Bullies fully vent their anger without retaliating, remembering that you control whether you accept their anger or are unaffected by it.*
2. *Confirm that you understand their side of the issue (using paraphrasing).*

3. *If they bully you in public, deal with them immediately. Don't wait until you have a private moment, as you would with other, less aggressive people.*
4. *Encourage them to obtain anger management.*

KNOW-IT-ALLS

They're "smart alecks" who brazenly claim to know much more about issues than they really do. They're knowledgeable individuals, but most of their information is based on assumptions, not facts. They're confident extroverts who are expert at promoting themselves. They can become battering rams when trying to get others to accept their ideas. They rebel against doing anything new if it's someone else's way, so they shut down when others give information. On the other hand, if it's their idea, they'll badger and coerce others until they give up in frustration. They don't listen to others, and are prone to interrupt others when they're in mid-sentence by starting an entirely new conversation. To overcome:

1. *Insist that they give you facts to back up their ideas.*
2. *Make sure the Know-it-all gives you a chance for input. Ask, "Is there any more information I need before I give my ideas?" This forces the person to listen to your side of the issue.*
3. *If they interrupt you, state, "I'm not finished yet. I gave you ample chance for you to express your ideas, now I'd like you to listen to mine."*

ALWAYS RIGHT

These people bring attention to themselves by defending their side of discussions in petty, noisy and angry ways that often embarrass others. They unreasonably expect others' agreement and act out of their firm belief that they are right. If you disagree with them, they'll badger you until you give in. They're immensely narrow-minded, with complete certainty that they know the only way to deal with the issue, and won't stop until they've convinced you to do things their way. They won't even contemplate implementing anyone else's ideas. These individuals do have their value: they force other group members not only to ensure that their ideas work, but to persist until their ideas are accepted. To overcome:

1. *When two or more ideas are presented, make sure that each idea's advantages and disadvantages are clearly identified. You might use a point system to determine the relevance of each idea.*
2. *Ideas must be backed up with facts, not assumptions.*
3. *If you are the presenter of the idea, use the stuck record technique (described at the end of this chapter) to ensure that your ideas are heard.*

CRITICIZERS/BROWBEATERS

They use sharp-pointed humor to provoke and goad you, and attempt to control a situation without being held accountable. They need an audience, such as the rest of the staff or a client. If others protest their antics, they claim their comments were supposed to be funny. To overcome:

1. *Ask repeatedly for clarification.*
2. *Shift their attention toward productivity.*
3. *Talk to them privately if the behavior continues.*

PICKY, PICKY, PICKY

They find fault with everything—are very negative-thinking people who may use vindictive sarcasm to provoke defensiveness in others. They nitpick and find fault with inconsequential matters. They insist on perfection for tasks that are not important. They won't let you forget past transgressions and harp on them at every opportunity. If problems arise, they're never at fault. They can be workaholics who have problems delegating tasks to others. Should they delegate a task, they constantly check on the work being completed. To overcome:

1. *Identify your concern about their negative-thinking attitude and ask them to work with you to correct their destructive behavior.*
2. *Encourage them to be more positive-thinking people by having them concentrate on the number of times they disagree with others and start sentences with the word, "but."*
3. *Redirect your energy into productive assignments.*
4. *Help them determine when perfection is and is not required.*

DOMINEERING/TYRANTS

Every conflict is a struggle for power. Only the strong survive, so you must fight to maintain your pecking order—which is at the top. They're tough, competitive and aggressive individuals who use others to get where they want to go. Everything in their life relates to power. They treat others with a high-handed, harsh and dictatorial manner. These too cause others to have the hair stand up on the back of their neck when they enter the room. To overcome:

1. *Have a meeting with them and use feedback to explain how their actions affect you and others. (Have examples of how the behavior negatively affected others.)*
2. *Explain that others would be far more cooperative if they were asked to do things rather than commanded to do them.*
3. *If this kind of behavior continues, point it out by stating "You're doing it again!"*

CONTROLLERS

They must be in charge of everything, be it at work or planning a picnic for their families. If things are going to be done right, they must be done by them—everyone else will do it incorrectly. To overcome: Same as "Domineering Tyrants."

TACKLERS

These people attack with a vengeance and you know they're after you, no holds barred. Most attacks happen in public, where the person seems to be defending their side of an issue. They're so determined to score points that they block whatever you toss out for consideration, and tackle you instead of the problem. They can trip you up, twisting what you say so that it has another meaning. They attack your credibility at every turn and are formidable opponents. To overcome:

1. *If they attack you personally, nudge them back to discussing the issue—not you. Don't let them goad you into making rash statements or actions. "We were discussing . . ."*

2. *Confront them privately if they continue to tackle you.*
3. *Concentrate on doing your job well, but be prepared for this individual to attack again.*

HOT HEADS

Others are forced to "walk on eggs" when around these individuals. They start arguments about anything and everything. They're real scrappers who treat you in a high-handed, harsh and dictatorial manner. They're abusive, abrasive and gluttons for power. They hog control— seldom delegate. A favorite tactic is to interrupt you in the middle of what you're saying. They're prone to assassinating your character (using labels) as they tear apart your remarks. To overcome:

1. *When they blow up unexpectedly, ask them why they're so angry. They won't expect this answer and often you can resolve an issue without retaliating.*
2. *If they interrupt you say, "I wasn't finished speaking. As I was saying . . ."*
3. *If they attack you in public, deal with them then and there. Defend yourself, using facts to back up your side of an issue (not emotions).*
4. *If you're their manager, let them know that this is unacceptable behavior and you'll have to put a written warning on their file if the behavior continues.*
5. *Encourage them to obtain help in handling their anger.*

BATTERING RAMS

No matter how much effort it takes or how much it costs, they insist that their way is the better way. Should others get in their way, they're stopped in their tracks. They bulldoze others, annihilating their perceived enemies and pressuring others to accept their ideas. They're not content to stay in their own ball park, but invade others' territory as well and expect their ideas to be accepted. To overcome:

1. *Put your foot down when anyone attempts to walk all over you. Let them know when they've overstepped their boundaries.*

2. *When the fault is at least partly yours, admit it.*
3. *Try not to lock horns. Explain: "I'm willing to listen to your side of the issue, if you're willing to listen to mine. Unless you give me that assurance, there's not much sense in us having this discussion."*

BOSSY

They order others around without having the authority to do so. They butt in where they have no right, and observers would think that they were the boss rather than the co-worker. They're highly critical of others, and invade their co-workers' territory. Although they're good workers, they won't tolerate those who work at a slower pace or take time to make decisions. Their co-workers are put off by their condescending behavior and constant criticism of their work. To overcome:

1. *Be sure to give them recognition when it's due.*
2. *Use feedback to explain what their actions are doing to others.*
3. *Encourage them to take a communication course so they can be less blunt and more tactful in their interaction with others.*
4. *If you're a manager and have tried several times without success to correct bossy behavior, explain that the behavior must change or you'll have to initiate disciplinary action.*

SLAVE DRIVERS

They may feel pressure from top management to do more, so they pass on these pressures to their staff. Many of these bosses are workaholics; some are perfectionists; most have a high energy level. They set a pace of work that's almost impossible for employees to meet. Even trainees are expected to work at top speed, even though they haven't been fully trained. This boss is too busy to answer questions and has the opposite of the open-door policy. They can be great delegators, and some sit back and watch their "busy bee" staff do all the work. To overcome:

1. *Determine whether you're really being overworked. Check your job description to determine the standards of performance set for your*

tasks. *If a job description with standards of performance is not available, ask for one so you'll know exactly what's expected of you.*

2. *Object if you find the standards of performance are unreasonable.*
3. *Let the boss know when you're in over your head. Do this by keeping "To Do" lists, with times required to complete each assignment.*

RULE BENDERS

They revel in breaking rules, cutting corners and finding easier ways to complete tasks. They break company rules by, for example, continually coming in late, saying they're sick (when they're actually on the golf course) and generally shirking their responsibilities. They do have their advantages because they can devise quicker, better ways of completing assignments, and detect duplication in business systems. To overcome:

1. *Clarify instructions on how tasks are to be completed, but be sure to look into their labor- or time-saving ideas.*
2. *Outline the consequences, should they try to bend the rules.*
3. *When rule-bending involves expense accounts, unless the exception can be proven, the employee pays for the extra expenses themselves.*

RIDICULERS

They're insensitive, inconsiderate people who deprecate you with heckling words that hide their real meaning. Some use sarcasm to voice their criticism, believing that this kind of humor will be easier for you to accept. Many of their humiliations and personal attacks take place in public so that others can clearly see they have a low opinion of you and your abilities. To overcome:

1. *Have a meeting and ask them to explain what they meant by their remarks.*
2. *If it was your boss who was criticizing you in public, state, "I have a problem and I need your help in solving it. Twice this week you've criticized me in public—once in front of my co-workers and the other day in front of a customer. I was very upset when you did this. In the future, could I ask you to wait until we have some privacy to discuss such matters?"*

PATRONIZERS

They make it clear that they have a low opinion of you by the condescending way they deal with you. They ask for your opinion, then ignore your ideas, interrupt you or zap you with putdowns as they dismiss your suggestions. Their distorted high opinion of themselves encourages them to degrade and devalue others, while giving the impression that they are special beings who have given you permission to be in their presence. They're insulting when they delegate tasks: *"This is an easy job—Pam can handle it."* To overcome:

1. *Remind yourself how good you really are.*
2. *If it's your boss, explain that you want to do a good job but find it difficult to do so because of their condescending behavior.*
3. *If it's a colleague, use feedback to identify what the patronizing behavior is doing to you.*

INTERRUPTERS

They rudely interrupt you in mid-sentence, often to start a new topic. They also interrupt you while you're trying to work. Bit by bit, they chip away at your time, keeping you from completing your assignments. They drop by your work station and expect you to discuss what they did on the weekend. When they leave, it's hard to regain your momentum after their interruption. They waste valuable time at meetings by having side conversations with others or asking non-relevant questions during presentations. When it's their turn to speak, they tend to ramble. To overcome:

1. *If you're interrupted, say, "I wasn't finished my statement before you interrupted me. As I was saying . . ."*
2. *Stop the rambler with sharply focussed comments and questions.*
3. *If they interrupt your work, explain why you can't be interrupted at that time.*
4. *Discourage interrupters from staying in your office by arranging to have your meetings with them in a boardroom, which enables you to end the meeting on your terms.*

5. *If the interruption is to discuss personal matters, tell them you'll talk to them later, at coffee or lunch break.*

SNOOPY/NOSEY

They eavesdrop on your conversations, and generally need to know every little bit of "dirt" so they can pass it on. They're excessively curious, intruding into matters that are none of their business. Whether it's in your home or your office, every piece of paper is picked up and read as if it were their own correspondence. They look over your shoulder when you're using the computer, and poke their noses into every crevice of your life. Most don't recognize how offensive their actions are perceived to be. While this quality can be an asset if they're researching a topic, it is seen as highly intrusive when they ask intensely personal questions. To overcome:

1. *Use feedback to explain how upsetting their behavior is, not only to you but to others.*
2. *Remember that just because someone asks a question, you don't have to answer. Say something like "I'd rather not talk about my personal life."*
3. *Don't let them entice you into exchanging gossip.*

EMPIRE BUILDERS

They'll use any sneaky tactic that enables them to bypass others and reach their goal of getting to the top. They have little interest in anyone else's progress unless they're seen as a threat. They will scare off, intimidate or destroy anyone who enters what they perceive as their "territory." Team playing is foreign to them, because of their need to receive attention and be "top dog." Their only loyalty to a company relates to the prestige their position gives them; once this changes, they move on. Their own needs always come first. To overcome:

1. *Have a talk with the Empire Builder to let them know that you won't tolerate any such behavior.*

2. *Make sure all members of the team have input and receive credit for their portions of assignments.*
3. *Initiate disciplinary action if Empire Builders overstep their boundaries, take advantage of others or appear to be stepping over others.*

"TOO BUSY"

They're always too busy to answer questions or supply what you need. To overcome:

1. *Clearly define the problems that occur when this happens.*
2. *If it's your manager who's too busy, remind him or her that a primary function of the position of manager is to make it easy for you to make him or her look good.*
3. *If it's a colleague, explain that he or she has become a bottleneck to your inability to complete your own work.*
4. *When approaching them with problems, supply at least two possible solutions.*
5. *If it's a staff member, help him or her choose priorities with red, orange and green tag system for assignments.*

STUBBORN

They won't budge no matter how convincing your argument. They're right and you're wrong, and nothing will make them believe otherwise. They will even dispute the facts you present to them, claiming they have been altered. They feel a need to control events, and if you disagree with them, they'll dig in even more, sticking tenaciously to their own way of doing things. To overcome:

1. *If this is your boss, know where he or she is coming from.*
2. *Present a substitute to their plan, identifying the pros and cons of your idea, and have them do the same with their own.*
3. *Act as though you expect acceptance.*
4. *If they won't budge, try to get their reasons in writing.*

DON JUANS

They're positive that the world thinks they're the world's most attractive human being. They strut and flaunt their sexuality to everyone, believing that they're attracted by their beauty or handsomeness rather than by their cocky attitude. To overcome:

1. *Give them recognition where it's due.*
2. *Watch for opportunities to explain how tiresome others find this trait.*
3. *Have them give reasons why they think they're so attractive.*

COMPETITORS/CHALLENGERS

In all facets of their lives, they compete with everyone and everything, turning every situation into a contest. They must win so that they can feel superior, and will give everything they have to make it happen. They seek and expect some kind of public announcement when they win, and will seek revenge on those who deny it to them. Should someone not accept their ideas, they feel as if they've failed, that they've been rejected personally. To overcome:

1. *Using feedback, explain what their actions are doing to you and others.*
2. *Explain how they can learn by really listening to others' ideas and building on them.*
3. *Encourage them to use their creativity to improve on existing ways of doing things.*
4. *Make sure you give them praise when praise is due.*

IMPOSERS

Their self-centered and exploitive nature allows them to impose their wishes and take advantage of others. They make promises that they have no intention of keeping. They could earn Academy Awards for their acting, because they have the ability to convince others that they're helpless and couldn't survive without assistance. They're so convincing, it's hard to say no. To overcome:

1. *Practice saying no until it becomes automatic.*
2. *Steel yourself to withstand their request for more and more input.*
3. *Explain what their actions do to those around them and that you object to being used by them.*

PREJUDICED

They make jokes at others' expense, some very openly, others very overtly. This prejudice can be against those of another race or color; someone fat or ugly, short or tall; or someone who has an accent or wears unusual clothes. To overcome:

1. *These types of "jokes" should be discouraged as soon as someone starts "Did you hear the one about a ..."*
2. *Use such reminders such as: "I didn't think that was funny."*
3. *Have a private session with the offender if necessary.*
4. *If you're their supervisor and they continue with this behavior, explain that the next time this happens you'll have to place a written warning in their personnel file.*

PERSISTENT

They pester others until they wear them down and get their way. They're determined to have their way—at any cost. To overcome:

1. *Use the stuck-record technique. (See end of this chapter.)*
2. *When you can't do what they want you to do, suggest alternatives.*
3. *If they persist, ask them why they're being so persistent (this is aggressive behavior and you have the right to say "no" and defend yourself).*

THIEVES

In this case we'll concentrate on those employees that take company supplies home from work. This can be anything as small as a couple of pencils to very expensive equipment. In some cases it is done to get back at management. Some of them will steal quantities far in excess of what they can ever use. To some extent, it's their way of getting around the rules and back at authority. Some may have passive/aggressive tendencies. To overcome:

1. *Have department managers monitor supplies and step in if something seems amiss.*
2. *Make sure company policies and procedures manuals outline what the penalty is should a staff member remove company property without permission.*
3. *If an employee takes company equipment from the workplace, they must have a signed document giving them permission to do so. This permission can be for 24 hours or for as long as the employee works for the company.*

NAME-CALLERS/LABELERS

When criticizing others, they call them names or label them, using such words as "stupid," "dumb," "crazy," "lazy," "bad" or "awkward." To overcome:

1. *If you are the receiver of the unfair criticism, ask them to be more specific: "Exactly what did I do that was wrong?"*
2. *Use feedback to describe how you feel when they label you or call you names.*

PASSIVE/AGGRESSIVE MANIPULATORS

These people can be very dangerous. They have a pathological reaction to authority and those they perceive are in positions of authority. They channel their aggression into passive behavior by slowing down efforts of others, and stonewall progress. They're very hard to detect, and others often feel frustrated when dealing with them but don't always understand why.

As most of us grow up, we're faced with restrictions that are normal and necessary. People with this tendency have often been controlled excessively, so the person learns to control others without confrontation. They love the thrill of insubordination, and it sometimes doesn't matter if they win, as long as it appears their opponents loose. They love to play win–lose games and put something over on others.

They use excuses such as: *"It's not my fault this didn't work; it's yours."* They show frequent signs of helplessness—the simplest thing seems beyond their comprehension. They provoke a feeling of defensiveness when others are dealing with them. Most tasks are performed late or not at all. When prodded they become argumentative. They're backstabbers and gossipers, and are often so good at it that others believe their falsehoods.

Most people display the signs noted above at one time or another. However, if this develops into being their normal behavior, these people are likely passive-aggressive, and others will have to remain on guard when dealing with them. Confront them using facts when you "catch them in the act." Make sure they understand the consequences of their actions: *"If this happens again, I'll ..."*

Some serious passive/aggressives have criminal tendencies. These people get a thrill out of speeding, of drinking and driving—and getting away with it. In some, this tendency keeps accelerating because they require higher and higher levels of danger, thrills and excitement to keep them appeased.

TANTRUMS

Adult tantrums are designed to cope with feelings of fear, helplessness and frustration. To a child, tantrums are a great equalizing mechanism. Such disruptive behavior continues into adulthood if the outbursts still work. However, tantrums produce a greater backwash of anger and resistance than any of the other difficult behaviors. Coping with a person having a tantrum is chiefly a matter of helping them regain self-control. To overcome;

1. *Give them time to run down and regain self-control.*
2. *Because tantrums are used to get attention, give them the opposite by saying, "I see you're very angry about this, I'll give you a chance to*

*calm down, then we can discuss this rationally." Then walk away
from them.*
3. *If they continue with this behavior, explain that their behavior is
unacceptable and you won't talk to them until they calm down.*
4. *Encourage them to obtain help in handling their anger.*

INTIMIDATORS

Whenever they don't get what they want, they use hidden ways to
threaten, coerce, hurt or embarrass others. Staff feel powerless when the
intimidator is their boss. They're noted for stabbing others in the back,
so don't drop your guard and be ready for an attack. To overcome:

1. *Prepare yourself psychologically for your next encounter.*
2. *Rehearse how you will respond the next time they try to intimidate you.*
3. *Walk away from them, explaining that their tactics aren't going to
work on you any more.*
4. *If this is your boss, call in reinforcements by speaking with someone
in the Human Resources Department, a mediator or an employee
relations manager. As a last resort, go above your boss's head to his
or her manager. Make sure you bring facts with you, not assumptions
and innuendoes. For example, "On Monday, my boss said . . . On
Tuesday he (she) did . . ."*
5. *If upper management won't help, write a letter of resignation, outlining in detail your reasons for leaving, then lodge a complaint of
harassment against your boss and the company.*

TIME-BOMBS

This type of individual attacks the person, not their ideas, often using
labels to indicate that their opponent is dumb, stupid or error-prone. If
others disagree with their ideas, they believe they're being criticized at
a personal level, so their attack is done with a vengeance. They have no
qualms about attacking others in public, and like to appear the victor.
However, as most observers have themselves been at the receiving end
of this person's actions, they're seldom taken in. To overcome:

1. *Use facts to defend your ideas instead of letting them goad you into making rash statements, over-reacting or reacting emotionally. Remember to keep your cool.*
2. *Confront them privately, warning them that if they continue to belittle you in public, you will be forced to retaliate.*
3. *Encourage them to obtain anger management training.*

SADISTS

They enjoy pointing out every fault and mistake you make, blowing small discrepancies out of proportion. They feel most powerful when they make others feel inferior. They love to criticize you in front of others—the bigger the audience, the better. They have a mean, vindictive streak. To overcome:

1. *Confront the Sadist, letting him or her know you won't tolerate manipulative behavior.*
2. *Use feedback to let them know what their behavior is doing to you and others.*
3. *If this person is your boss and their bad behavior persists, speak first to upper management. If they won't stop the behavior, write a letter of resignation, outlining in detail your reasons for leaving, then lodge a complaint of harassment against your boss and the company.*

REVENGERS

These people take everything personally and make sure others are "paid back" for any perceived mistreatment. They deeply resent how they've been mistreated, and feel cheated or neglected. Their grudges can continue for years, wasting valuable time and energy. Some never forgive others, still plotting revenge against their enemies on their deathbed. To overcome:

1. *Remember that the other person has control over your life as long as you're wasting your valuable time and energy plotting revenge.*
2. *If you can't do something about the issue right away, let it go. The adage "what goes around, comes around" is true in this case.*

3. *Trust that the above will occur. Just stand back and watch it happen, with no waste of energy on your part. Know that somehow they will be paid back for their transgression, without you having to do anything.*
4. *If you can't remove your desire for revenge, obtain anger management training.*

ZEALOTS

They're extremists who have a very biased view of what's right and wrong. They zealously commit themselves, without weighing all the facts. They're bossy, arrogant people who let their biases overshadow their sense of reason. They see a problem, put their heads down and go full bore into solving the problem without weighing the consequences. They can run off a cliff because they fail to visualize what will happen after they solve their problem. Their solutions often cause more problems, which can have serious repercussions. To overcome:

1. *Before starting projects, ask them for details of their planning strategy that includes all stages, and to identify what they expect to accomplish.*
2. *Press them for details such as how their ideas compare with another's (pros and cons).*

BACK-STABBERS

These are two-faced individuals who knife you in the back while acting friendly to your face. Much of their work is done behind your back and without your knowledge. Should you trust them with confidential information, they betray that trust; this is done so they can have control over you, and to get ahead in life. As others learn about their abusive behavior, they can become very lonely people. To overcome:

1. *Expect them to use this behavior, and be prepared for their actions.*
2. *Confront them when you catch them in the act.*
3. *Watch your back, and don't discuss matters you wouldn't want repeated.*

WHEELER-DEALERS

These foxy, sly, cunning people try to maneuver others in any way possible. They're smart because they aren't openly aggressive. Some even start a problem so they can reap the benefit that goes with providing a solution. Through devious means, they manipulate others into doing things they had no intention of doing. Many are physically attractive and use their sex appeal to wheel and deal. To overcome: *Use the technique for "Back-stabbers."*

SET YOU UP TO FAIL

These people promise but seldom deliver, leaving you holding the bag. They're company bottlenecks who withhold important information you need to complete assignments. This isn't done because they procrastinate, but because they know how crucial the information is to your success or failure. They want you to fail. Most of them are in direct competition with you for a promotion, and will do anything to see that they, not you, get the advancement. You seldom see their treachery until the deed is done. Their attack can be more serious than that of a Back-stabber, because it's harder to see it coming in time to defend yourself. To overcome:

1. *Put everything in writing when dealing with this individual.*
2. *Let them know that you're on to them. With facts, identify how their behavior affected the outcome of the assignment or project.*
3. *No matter how charming they are, keep your guard up and watch your back!*

INSTIGATORS

These are real agitators—experts at twisting the truth and provoking others. They make hateful comments, inciting conflict that causes morale problems. Some are overqualified for their jobs and stir up trouble through sheer boredom. They're the ones who instigate union action against management; who help others lodge wrongful-dismissal charges; who fight when someone doesn't get the promotion they expected. They make waves and do anything to stir up trouble. To overcome:

1. *Keep them busy. Use their high energy for productive ends.*
2. *Warn them about their unacceptable behavior, explaining the consequences should they persist in it.*
3. *Those who are overqualified for their jobs: explain that until they improve their performance in their existing position, they won't be considered for a promotion.*

CONNIVERS

Conniving bosses give a verbal set of instructions about how they wish you to complete an assignment, then blame you if it fails. They may change the way they want you to complete an assignment three or four times so that, if it does fail, they can complain that you didn't do what they wanted you to do. To overcome:

1. *Obtain instructions in writing. If they're given verbally, make notes, then confirm that this is the way he or she wants the assignment completed.*
2. *Put everything in writing. Use memos that have a section for a reply, to keep both pieces of information together.*
3. *Make sure you have an accurate, up-to-date job description with standards of performance so you're clear about what is expected of you.*

DEFIERS

These insubordinate employees buck authority figures, and oppose all changes to established policies and procedures. They insist on completing assignments their own way. If procedures are changed, they resist and emphatically challenge the new way. Even after they're forced to start using the new system, they'll slowly but surely return to doing it their own way. If they're new employees, they bend over backwards trying to convince the company that their way is the best. To overcome:

1. *Check your own attitude to determine whether your way is truly better.*
2. *Let the Defier get their gripe off their chest.*

3. *Set guidelines, using a detailed, up-to-date job description with standards of performance.*
4. *Decide how you will deal with the employee should they defy again.*

PRIMA DONNAS

They're similar to "Don Juan" personalities. These temperamental, moody, demanding, short-fused individuals expect special treatment. They have a high regard for their skills and abilities, and try to manipulate others into believing they're indispensable. They were likely spoiled as children and have learned how to get what they want in life. They're persistent and cagey, and prone to giving ultimatums. As a customer or client, they can drive companies to distraction with their expectations of special service. To overcome:

1. *If the Prima Donna is an employee, call their bluff. Learn to say no when necessary.*
2. *Use feedback to explain how others must feel when they use such behavior.*
3. *Expect them to fulfill their obligations, with no special treatment.*
4. *If they're a client, give them only what they deserve, and say no when applicable.*

BRAIN-PICKERS

They're exploitive individuals who steal others' ideas and take credit for them. They pick your brain under the ruse that they're your friend, until they obtain the information they were seeking; then you don't hear from them again until you learn that they've stolen your ideas and are taking credit for them. To overcome:

1. *Be on guard. Don't reveal anything you think they will use to their advantage or against you.*
2. *Evade small talk when conversing with Brain-pickers.*
3. *Put your ideas down on paper, and make sure someone in authority is aware of new ideas you're investigating.*

SUPER-SENSITIVE

These people make others "walk on eggs" because they never know when this person might take offense or erupt. They're exceptionally sensitive and take every critical comment as a personal attack. Many resort to tantrums to get their side heard. They suffer from very low self-esteem and are subject to becoming hurt at the least hint of disapproval from others. To overcome:

1. *Help them build self-confidence.*
2. *Help them recognize when they're over-reacting.*
3. *Suggest they receive anger management counseling and assertiveness training.*

UNETHICAL

No matter what the cost, ethical or otherwise, they must get their way. They cheat on their income tax, buy radar detectors, use illegal television receivers and so on. They get a charge out of cheating others and getting away with it. They spend much of their time in court fighting legal battles. Many of their adversaries throw their hands in the air because of all the time and effort it takes to bring them to justice, which just spurs this kind of person on to do it again. To overcome:

1. *Show them your company's code of ethics.*
2. *Point out what the consequences will be if they repeat their "error."*
3. *If they have broken the law, insist they make restitution.*
4. *If the infraction is serious enough, lay criminal charges and terminate the employee immediately.*

OTHER MANIPULATORS

These people don't really fit into any of the other categories. Their personalities can shift as they go from being up-front individuals to those who manipulate predominantly in circumstances where they feel they're not in control. We've all fit these categories from time to time, but we were still using manipulation.

PROCRASTINATOR

These people always have excuses as to why a job isn't done. They say, *"I'll do it tomorrow,"* which may or may not come to pass. People can tell that procrastination is becoming a problem when they have something important to do, not much time to do it in, but find themselves looking for other things to do instead. Or when they set deadlines and don't meet them; constantly delay making important decisions, or working furiously at the last minute to complete crucial assignments. To overcome.

1. *Encourage them to do the distasteful tasks first.*
2. *Slot those kinds of activities into the high-energy part of their day.*
3. *Help them set deadlines and enforce them.*
4. *Be sure to outline the consequences should this practice continue in the future.*

ALWAYS LATE

They're late for events they don't want to attend or aren't ready when others are. They disrupt meetings, social events, concerts, and are generally lacking in consideration for others' valuable time. To overcome:

1. *Explain clearly how offensive this behavior is to you and others—that others feel that the behavior signifies that others' time is worthless and that only their time is important.*
2. *Help them identify situations where being late has had serious repercussions.*

ALWAYS SLOW

Sure their report is ready, but it took them so long to prepare it that the boss felt like taking over for them. These are low-energy people who appear to be "putting in time"—existing rather than living—usually in jobs they don't like. They can drive other more organized people to distraction by being late for work, meetings and appointments. They may feel insecure about their abilities and try to forestall the results by being late. Wasting time over trifling matters, they loiter and linger. They are great fence-sitters because they can't reach decisions. It's better, they tell themselves, to gather ALL the facts, and hear from everyone, before starting. Or they move from one task to another, never completing anything. To overcome:

1. *Make sure they have job descriptions that clearly identify their areas of responsibility.*
2. *Don't cover up for the dawdler. Explain how you feel when they keep you waiting.*
3. *Teach dawdlers to be punctual.*
4. *If you're to meet them for lunch, wait for them ten minutes, then order lunch.*
5. *If you have to pick them up, wait five minutes and, if they're not ready, go without them.*

SLOPPY OR CARELESS

The work is done so poorly that someone else has to re-do the effort, which often takes more time than the original task. They're unconcerned that their negligence might affect others. These are people who are capable of doing the task but, for some reason, don't want to perform. To overcome:

1. *Demonstrate concern for them as individuals, using feedback to explain what their actions are doing to undermine their work production.*
2. *If you're on a team with them, make sure it's clearly stated that they're responsible for their portion of the assignment.*
3. *Don't cover for them when they fail to perform.*

FORGETFULNESS OR NEGLECT

Their usual comment is *"I forgot."* They expect others to remind them of things they should do, deadlines that are set, who's responsible for what project. *"Oh, I thought you were looking after that!"* To overcome:

1. *Put information about assignments in writing.*
2. *At meetings, when they promise to do something, have a wrap-up at the end of the meeting in which each participant confirms what he or she is to do before the next meeting. This way meeting members can't say they weren't responsible for their part.*

IMPULSIVES

When they tackle problems, they act first and think later. After they're well into solving the problem, they stop to figure things out; that's when they realize that they're tackling the wrong problem and waste considerable time and effort in backtracking. Observers of their activity see a whirlwind of action but aren't sure what they're trying to accomplish, and so are unable to stop their activities or direct them toward the right solution. Their problem-solving often fails, which can result in two problems rather than one. To overcome:

1. *Ask them for a written plan.*
2. *Encourage them to itemize, step by step, how they're going to accomplish each task.*
3. *Ask them to identify obstacles they might run into.*
4. *Ensure that they have all the required information before they make their decisions.*

CLANNISH

These people seek support in numbers. They find power by banding together in a group. These are not simply friends or co-workers who find they have a lot in common, but workers who stick together to cause trouble and buck authority. They have a leader who makes most of the decisions for them and whom they follow blindly. Their sheer numbers can overwhelm and intimidate those in command. To overcome (for bosses):

1. *Make every effort to get the leader on your side by explaining the benefits to them of working with you rather than against you.*

2. *Dissolve threatening groups by relocating offenders and discouraging socializing.*
3. *Give them group projects that require the joint effort of several people who work well together.*

PERFECTIONISTS

These people feel that everything, no matter how trivial, must be done perfectly. They're worriers who expect too much from themselves and keep polishing their work to meet their excessively high expectations. They keep putting off finishing assignments. The more they worry, the less they produce. If they're bosses, unfortunately some expect the same perfectionist behavior from their staff. To overcome:

1. *Using feedback, help perfectionists deal with reality.*
2. *Reassure them that not everything has to be perfect.*
3. *Help them with time management.*

RAMBLERS

They ramble on, taking up everyone's valuable time. They seldom take the time to think before they speak, so their conversation jumps from one thing to another, leaving the listener either "tuned out" or wondering what's their point? They recite idle prattle, meaningless stories of little interest to you or others. Because people run from them, they can be very lonely people, not comprehending that their talkativeness is what makes others shun their company. They very much want your admiration and assume you want to share all their interests and experiences. To overcome:

1. *Have the person prepare for your discussion by putting ideas down on paper.*
2. *Throughout your conversation with them, use paraphrasing to confirm their pertinent information.*
3. *If they don't respond to feedback about their behavior, tactfully remind them by saying, "We're getting off track. We were discussing . . ."*

SOCIALIZERS

They have a strong need to socialize and choose to make personal visits or phone calls rather than complete their work. They're in their element at cocktail parties and are wonderful networkers. They have trouble getting down to business, and give the impression that life is wasted unless they're having fun. They're very friendly and congenial, so they are ecstatic if you ask them to plan office social affairs. However, they'll procrastinate and interrupt others' work rather than buckle down and do their own. To overcome:

1. *Make sure they have an accurate, up-to-date job description with standards of performance so they know exactly what's expected of them.*
2. *Discourage desk-hopping and spending company money on non-work-related matters. Be alert, and correct such behavior as it happens.*
3. *Initiate disciplinary action if their behavior continues.*

BOTTLENECKS

They dawdle and waste time while you wait for their work so you can complete your own. They put off asking for the help they need and consequently delay everyone else. Bottlenecks occur whenever people fail to take essential action, whether because of indecision, laziness, mistaken priorities, stubbornness, overwork, or simply because they procrastinate. To overcome:

1. *Make sure they know the kinds of problems that are occurring because they're dragging their feet.*
2. *Give them plenty of lead-time before deadlines.*
3. *If their inaction continues, go to a higher authority, or start disciplinary measures if you're their supervisor.*

CLOCK-WATCHERS

Come five o'clock, they're gone. They refuse new assignments by saying, *"That's not in my job description."* They play truant and find any excuse not to work or attend meetings. Many hate their jobs and have the ability to do much more complex work, but won't take steps to alleviate the situation. They often badmouth their company and its products, and tell everyone how much they hate their job. They can't wait for their work-day to be over so they can bowl, golf or do something else that stimulates them. To overcome:

1. *Explain what their actions are doing to their promotional opportunities.*
2. *Suggest that they obtain career counseling to determine the kind of work they should be doing.*
3. *If they decide to stay, create more challenges, excitement and pride in their work.*

UNSOCIABLE

They're reclusive, introverted, aloof and uninterested in others. They can appear cold and uncaring, giving an *"I want to be alone"* impression. Some use this attitude deliberately to try to intimidate you, but most are not out to alarm or conquer you. They're not concerned about you; they are merely aloof, unaffectionate people. They're much more comfortable working alone and are agitated if forced to work closely with others. Most are very detail-oriented, not people-oriented. To overcome:

1. *Remember, this is their problem, not yours. They don't normally mean to offend.*
2. *If you're their boss, ensure that they have a job which allows them to work alone.*

WORKAHOLICS

They hide from their problems by immersing themselves in work. Others become workaholics out of necessity. To overcome:

1. *Decide whether they have a "Type A" personality that needs to be busy all the time. If so, don't fret—this is just the way they like it to be.*

2. *Encourage them to delegate more if the work is overwhelming.*
3. *Encourage them to prioritize their work and to make "To Do" lists.*
4. *For one week, ask them to itemize what they do with their time (at and away from work) and make adjustments accordingly.*

NEGATIVIST

They're the ones who constantly use phrases such as *"That won't work"* or *"It's no use trying"* or *"We tried that already and it didn't work."* The cup is always half empty, not half full. To overcome:

1. *Encourage them to confide in a friend.*
2. *Help them change their attitude.*
3. *Before trying something new, encourage them to ask two questions: What have I got to gain? What have I got to lose?*
4. *Ask them whether they like being around other negative-thinking people.*

BORED

They're in a rut, and intend on staying in it. However, they spend much of their time complaining about the little things in life that irritate them. They're envious of others who get ahead in life, but don't seem to find the necessary tools or energy to do the same for themselves. To overcome:

1. *Encourage them to write down their lifetime personal and career goals.*
2. *Ask them whether they like the work they're doing. If they don't, ask them what they'd rather be doing.*
3. *Help them set goals to make it happen.*
4. *See "Whiners, Complainers and Bellyachers."*

LUCKY

They assume that you have what you have, because you're "lucky"— not because of any hard work on your behalf. They gamble and expect that, if they're lucky enough, they'll get what they want out of life. To overcome: Same as "Bored" except #4.

MUMBLER

They have never learned how to articulate their words so that each word is understood on its own. Everything they say runs together, forcing others to ask them to repeat themselves or they're simply misunderstood. To overcome:

1. *Encourage them to take speech training or voice lessons.*
2. *Explain how frustrating it is to have to listen so hard to what they say.*
3. *If their voice is soft, encourage them to project their voices.*

VAGUE

They are the opposite of analytical. When pressed for details, they're unable to provide them. They talk in generalities rather than specifics. To overcome:

1. *Teach them how to research a topic so they can be more specific with their information.*
2. *Have them itemize the steps they will take to complete tasks.*
3. *Have them write a description of what happened at your latest meeting, then critique and ask for more details of items described.*

TERRITORIAL

These people are fanatical about what they believe is their territory. They'll fight anyone who attempts to enter their territory or doesn't show homage to their ownership. This territory includes their cars, their office, their desk, their clothing and even their pens. To overcome:

1. *Recognize that the person feels threatened—that's why they feel so defensive.*
2. *They probably feel as if you have invaded their "space."*
3. *Different cultures have different ideas about personal body space.*

4. *Reassure the person that you have no intention of invading his or her space and apologize if you've done so in the past.*

MONOTONOUS

These people never have much to say. Ask them, *"What's new?"* and their inevitable answer is *"Nothing."* They make others do all the talking, seldom ask questions or contribute to the conversation. These are not shy people, but people who plod along day after day doing the same thing every day. To overcome:

1. *Invite them to an exciting event.*
2. *Include them in activities.*
3. *Have them take their turn arranging an exciting evening or weekend activity.*
4. *Get them involved in helping others, which might get them out of their shell.*

DAYDREAMERS

We all daydream, but some do it to excess—to a point where it interferes with work or productivity. It's not always fair to pin the blame for daydreaming on them. Their job or their life might be so boring that they can't keep their minds occupied. Machine-like functions tend to create opportunities for daydreaming. To overcome:

1. *Check the design and decor of their work area.*
2. *Think about implementing a job-rotation system.*
3. *Give employees more input into how they complete their tasks.*

MESSY

What appears to be messy to you might not be to others. Could you be the problem, because you're a perfectionist? Or are they *really* messy? With some, their mothers always picked up after them, or they grew up in a messy home. This mess does not bother them at all, so they might be surprised when you point this out to them. To overcome:

1. *Set a good example.*
2. *Point out the problems their messiness has caused.*
3. *Have a written checklist of housekeeping activities. Make sure their work area is left clean at the end of the day.*

HYPERACTIVE

These whirlwinds wear everybody out just watching them in action. They're seldom still, talk a mile a minute, and have their fingers in at least ten pies at once. Their nervous energy can be passed on to everyone else, which raises everyone's stress levels. To overcome:

1. *Remind the hyperactive person to relax.*
2. *Explain how their constant activity is making everyone edgy.*
3. *Keep them busy. Use their energy wisely, in activities that will channel their energies positively.*

ANALYTICAL

They analyze and pick apart everything in their path. In a conversation, they need to know every detail. Superficial conversations do not exist for analytical people. Others may feel as if they're being grilled. To overcome:

1. *Ask them why they need so much detail.*
2. *Explain how annoying it is when they expect too much information.*
3. *Utilize their analytical abilities by giving them research assignments.*

STINGY

These people are so possessive of their time, their money and their possessions that they find it very difficult to part with any of them. Many come from a background where they had little money, so had to do without replacement items. Therefore, they hoard and keep their belongings, rather than share them. They're often labeled "tightwads" because of their frugal nature. To overcome:

1. *Encourage them to pay their way.*
2. *Be meticulous when settling joint bills because they will likely pay for less than their share.*

If you find you're using these manipulative ploys—stop and figure out how you could deal with the issue in a more direct or honest manner.

Avoiding Ambiguous Messages

Sometimes our words and behavior are open to more than one interpretation. If we don't realize this and clarify our intended meaning, our behavior can be misinterpreted. Here's an example:

1. *Supervisor's Intention.* A supervisor wants to let Mary (one of his staff) know that he recognizes and appreciates the extra load she's been carrying lately. He debates which of the following would best communicate his appreciation:
   a. giving Mary some time off;
   b. taking Mary out to lunch;
   c. telling Mary how he feels;
   d. trying to reduce Mary's workload.
2. *Supervisor's Action.* He decides on d, and eases up on Mary's workload.
3. *Mary's Reaction.* Mary notices the reduced workload, but doesn't know what it means. Her supervisor might be:
   a. criticizing her for not having kept up with her workload;
   b. trying to tell her she shouldn't spend so much time on the phone;
   c. trying to be helpful;
   d. convinced she can't handle crisis situations.
4. *Effect on Mary.* She decides it's a, and feels hurt and put down.
5. *Mary Encodes:* I'm not going to let him know that he's hurt me. Shall I:
   a. say nothing?
   b. say thanks?
6. *Mary's Action.* She decides to say thanks.

7. *Effect on Supervisor.* He believes that Mary understands and appreciates what he's done.

This is a classic example of how ambiguous behavior can be misunderstood. The supervisor's intention was positive and caring. However, the effect on his employee was the direct opposite of what he wanted. How much better it would have been if he had backed his actions up with words. By using positive feedback, he would have made sure Mary knew why he was easing her workload.

The following example illustrates the sometimes serious consequences that can result from failure to explain ambiguous behavior. A company was doing well, even though the economy was down. The company had decided to move its facilities to a larger, more comfortable building. The good news was to be announced to employees at a special meeting planned for 5:00 p.m. Thursday. The problems began when workers from another company came to the reception desk Monday morning. They told the receptionist that they were there to measure the offices. When asked why, they explained, "Because the new owners need this information before they move in."

After checking with her office manager, the receptionist gave permission to the workers to measure the offices. She began having the awful feeling that she might be out of a job soon. At coffee break, she mentioned the situation to two other co-workers, who of course passed this information on to others. By Tuesday afternoon, word reached the company executives that half their staff were applying for jobs with other companies and thought Thursday's meeting would announce the folding of their company. Management quickly decided to announce the good news on Tuesday at 5:00 p.m.

Dealing with Persistent People

In this age of telemarketing, we've all encountered telephone salespeople. For example, you're probably familiar with the sweet young thing who wants to explain her company's rug-cleaning special. When she identifies herself and asks how your day is going, you know that a sales pitch will follow. I suggest using the following technique:

THE STUCK RECORD

"We have a special on rug cleaning today."

"Thank you for calling, but I'm not interested."

"But this special is just good for this week ..."

"I'm not interested."

"How about having your living-room suite cleaned?"

"I'm not interested. . . . Goodbye." You hang up.

Many might feel that this person is just trying to make a living. My answer to this is that they're invading my privacy. If I want rug cleaning, I'll call and ask for it.

With the stuck-record technique, you simply repeat the same thing over and over again. You don't raise your voice, or get defensive. By the third refusal, the salesperson usually accepts that you're serious.

This technique also works well in an office if you're the one who has to fend off salespeople. Let's say your instructions are to accept only a person's business card and catalog (or information on their product). Someone from your company will follow up if the offered product or service is of interest.

Here's how to handle the next salesperson:

"I'd like to see the office manager please."

"Do you have an appointment?"

"No, I don't."

"Could you please tell me the reason for your visit?"

"I'd like to explain our product to your office manager."

"My instructions are to accept any information you'd care to leave. The office manager will call you if she's interested."

"Our special is only on this week."

"Leave the information with me, and the office manager will call you if she's interested."

"I'm sure she would want to see me."

"Leave the information with me, and the office manager will call you if she's interested [you hold out a hand for the information]. Thank you."

You can use this technique in other situations too—for instance, when someone is trying to convince you to do something you really don't want to do.

"Harry, can you drive me home from work tonight?"

"No I can't, sorry. I'm busy."

"Harry, I really need you to drive me home from work tonight. How come you can't drive me?"

"As I said, I'm too busy."

When anyone asks you to explain why you've said no, they're acting aggressively and are trying to take advantage of you. You're under no obligation to tell people why you can't do what they want you to do. Use this technique whenever you want to say no to somebody who's trying to convince you to say yes. No guilt feelings!

4

DEALING WITH DIFFICULT CLIENTS

GENERAL PRINCIPLES AND TECHNIQUES

For some of us the most difficult and exasperating people we encounter are clients and customers. Companies usually forbid their employees to retaliate when faced with clients' negative behavior. The result is often frustrated, stressed-out employees.

Those who work on the front lines, representing their company, are susceptible to losing their cool. This is especially true if they have to deal on the phone or in person with angry or dissatisfied clients. Clients who have a beef may be irritable, rude, impatient, persistent, emotional or aggressive. They often choose a representative of the company (possibly *you*) as the butt of their anger. How you handle their problem makes all the difference to how both of you feel. Let's put ourselves in the customer's place for a minute.

Customer Service

Like you and me, customers appreciate courtesy in the service provided to them. One thing employees may forget is that "The customer is always number 1." Some employees give the impression that looking after a client is an interruption to their real work. Such behavior implies that the employee is doing clients a favor by helping them. In reality, the customer's needs should take precedence over any other work the employee has.

Unfortunately, many people are employed in the service industry simply "because the job was available." These people should be employed elsewhere. If you work in the service industry, ask yourself, "Do I enjoy serving people? Do I want to make their day better than it was before they met me?" If the answer is no—get out of the service industry!

One goal society should have is to create a way of life that allows people to serve others without feeling subservient.

Some men may feel that serving others (either at home or on the job) is demeaning or "women's work." They believe they'll lose their masculinity if they serve others.

Your tone of voice and body language give you away. There's a tremendous difference between starting a conversation with a curt "Yes?" and smiling while saying, "Good morning, how can I help you today?" In a department-store study, I found that six out of ten clerks never smiled. They gave the impression they were doing customers a favor by waiting on them.

Customer service isn't just important for those who work in stores and restaurants. Every kind of organization that exists in society needs proper customer service. Rudeness, impatience and insensitivity aren't compatible with good, professional sales. Even so, salespeople display many of these negative traits for a wide range of reasons. Discourtesy, disrespect, indifference, slow service, ignorance of the services offered by the company, errors and negative behavior repel customers and leave bad feelings. Customers often respond to the bad feelings by simply staying away.

Customers gravitate to places where they get the most positive feelings. The way employees act with customers is far more important than all the company money spent on advertising and image-building.

How can you improve customer service? If you spend time thinking about ways you can give better service and make customers happier, you'll achieve success wherever you work.

The most successful members of service organizations share common traits. They learn everything they possibly can about their organization and how it can serve its clients better. *Knowledgeable employees know:*

- what their organization does;
- who their key personnel are;
- why the organization works the way it does;
- what service or product the organization offers;
- what common questions or problems are likely to arise;
- how they can help clients most effectively.

Successful employees also manage to find out what customers want, expect and need. They go out of their way to do this by asking questions and really listening to the answers. They anticipate questions about the product or service the company offers.

Do you listen to your customers and honestly try to help them? Keep them informed about what you're doing to meet their needs? Let them know exactly what to anticipate? People almost always accept accurate estimates or honest reasons for delays.

You may think of your job as dull and routine, but you insult your clients if you make them feel as if they're not important or if you look bored with your job. Clients stop buying or switch their buying habits if salespeople don't make the buying experience a pleasant one.

Again trying to put yourself in the customer's place, consider for a moment whether you've encountered the following situations in the past:

- You're five years old, and you've been waiting at the ice cream counter watching much taller people (who came in after you) being served before you.
- You go into a restaurant, sit down and watch others being served. Some people who came in after you are halfway through their meal before your order is taken.
- You go into a department store and stand quietly while the clerks have a little chit-chat before acknowledging you.
- You get gas and have your oil checked. Later you find that the attendant has left oily fingerprints all over your newly washed car.
- You've booked a room, but receive skeptical looks from the front-desk clerk, who can't find your hotel reservation.

- It's raining heavily and you struggle with a rental car released without windshield-washer fluid.
- You order from room service at 7:00 a.m. and have to do without your breakfast because it doesn't arrive before you have to leave for an 8:30 meeting.
- You're short of cash so you write a check to yourself. You present it to a teller of your own bank where you're a regular customer. The teller gives you a suspicious look and demands two pieces of personal identification.

I'm sure many of these examples strike a chord with you. Companies should be more aware that a poorly served customer may never come back to use their services. It amuses me to see businesses spending huge sums to get customers back who might never have left if they'd received better service and a little courtesy. That is all your clients expect of you as well.

Real damage is caused when customers storm out of the shop. Not only do many not come back, but they tell all their friends about the poor service, too. If an angry customer comes to you for help, you have the ideal opportunity to prevent that damage. The real disaster hasn't happened yet. If you handle the situation correctly, it won't happen. Remember, once you've lost a customer, it's twice as hard to get him or her back.

Have you ever left a store (even though you wanted to buy something) simply because you were not able to get proper service? If customers know they will receive good service, they may be prepared to pay more for an item or accept a substitute for their first choice.

When I'm dissatisfied with service or don't get what I require from a company, I feel I have two choices: (a) I can decide never to go back, or (b) I can give them a second chance.

I've learned to give companies a second chance by complaining to someone who's in a position to correct the situation.

I had received poor service with an airline. Instead of making my travel arrangements with another airline (a definite alternative), I chose to speak to the supervisor of the offending ticket agent. I explained my dilemma to the supervisor, who made the following comment: "If you're happy with our airline—tell everyone. If you're dissatisfied with our service, please tell me—because I'm in a position to do something about it!" He promised to speak to his employee about the problem.

Here are a few situations that may have happened to you. See what you would do:

1. You work for a company that supplies auto parts. You're waiting on clients at the front desk, and a man rushes in. He knows that you're dealing with another customer. He gives the impression that he's in a hurry by shifting his weight from foot to foot, looking at his watch and sighing. How can you make his wait a little easier?

Remember that there's nothing more frustrating than waiting impatiently for a person to assist you who doesn't seem to know you're there. Your first step should be to acknowledge the client's presence. You can do this by saying, "I'll be with you in a moment."

2. You finish with your original client. You nod to the man, and he comes up to the counter. What should you say to him, to make him feel better about having to wait?

Say, "Thank you for your patience. What can I do for you today?"

3. The client shows you a form he has completed that he received in the mail. But someone has sent the wrong order form to him. You explain that it's the wrong form, and he becomes very angry. What should you reply?

Your first impulse might be to say, "Well, I wasn't responsible for sending you the wrong form" (defending yourself), or "George must have sent it by mistake" (blaming someone else). Would that make him happy? Of course not! He doesn't care who sent him the wrong form, he just wants his car parts!

What you should say is, "I'm sorry you received the wrong form. I don't blame you for being upset, I would be too if that had happened to me. Let me help you fill out the correct form."

In this transaction, you didn't pass the buck. Not only have you apologized for the error and empathized with the person, but you've taken active steps to correct the problem.

4. Suppose it was you who sent the wrong form to him? Do you say, "We've just changed our system, and we don't use that form any more" (passing the buck)? Or do you admit your error? "I'm sorry, I

made a mistake. This is the form I should have sent to you. Let me save you some time by helping you fill it out."

Dealing with Frustrated Clients

Here are some of the frustrations (which can lead to anger) clients and customers have identified:

Need	*Block*	*Satisfaction of Need*
	NO ONE LISTENS TO ME. SOMETHING WENT WRONG. I'M NOT GETTING YOUR HELP. THE PRODUCT DOESN'T WORK.	

Your first step should be to determine what the customer's block is. Then you can concentrate on the problem.

If clients believe that "No one listens to me," and take out their frustration by shouting at you, how can you show them that you're listening? Your body language would show this and you would paraphrase what you believe they have said. Then you would ask questions to learn more about their problem. This would also assist in dealing with "something went wrong," "I'm not getting your help" and "the product doesn't work."

Dealing with Angry Clients

Remind yourself that angry clients probably have a need that isn't being met and believe you have the ability to at least start the problem on the way to being solved. However, you may find it more effective *not* to focus immediately on solving the problem.

First, Deal with the Clients' Feelings. Use empathy—put yourself in their shoes. Say such things as, "I don't blame you for being upset. I'd feel that way too if that had happened to me." Listen carefully, maintaining eye contact, nodding your head, and giving other signs of being attentive. Ask questions to clarify matters for yourself: "And then what happened?" or "Did the item not fit properly?" Then give the client feedback on what you understand the problem (or cause of anger) to be.

Then, Deal with Their Problem. Once you've dealt with clients' feelings, you're now ready to deal with their problem. Find out what they want from you. Say something like, "I see we have a problem here. *What would you like me to do to help you?*" Many employees forget to ask this question, but it is a very powerful problem-solving tool. Often clients don't really know what they want from you. You should then clarify what is really being requested and take steps to solve the problem.

What could you say if you can't do what the person wants? If you just tell someone that you can't meet his or her needs, the person will be understandably unhappy. However, if you can offer alternatives, the person will be less unhappy. Whenever you can't meet a client's needs, tell the person what you *can* do that comes closest to meeting the need. Give the person at least two alternatives, but not more than three. (Any more than three is confusing.) What you've done is return the control of the situation to the client. In the client's mind, he or she is now back in the "driver's seat." The result is a win–win situation.

If there aren't any alternatives, explain the company rules and/or policies that make it impossible to meet the client's request. Explain only what's applicable to the person's own situation. Then work with the client to come up with a course of action (or an alternative you've suggested) so you both understand what's to happen. Make sure you follow up and do what you've said you'll be doing. Give the personal finishing touch (tender loving care) by urging customers to contact you should they have problems in the future.

NOTE: Keep in mind that all problems aren't this easy to solve. You may not be able to satisfy customers fully, but you can try to negotiate with them so there's no winner or loser.

Correcting Your Own Mistakes

What can you do when *you* made the mistake? First, don't be ashamed to admit it. Then state, "I'm sorry that happened. Let's see what I can do to correct the error." Then correct your mistake. Don't feel you have to defend yourself with such statements as, "We've been frantically busy. That's why I made a mistake." Whatever you do, don't ignore the problem; that will just compound the client's anger at both you and your company.

Do you have a problem admitting that you made a mistake? We all make mistakes, and most of us hate to admit it. But when someone makes a mistake and acknowledges it, doesn't your respect for that person go up? Most people wrongly assume that others will respect them less if they admit to a mistake. The opposite is true. You've blundered, you've admitted it and you're willing to fix the problem. It works far better that way for both of you. If the client continues to argue, say, "What would you like me to do to solve this problem?"

Using the "Stuck-Record" Technique

I have to enforce rules and regulations to my clients. They don't like many of these rules, and I feel pressured when they insist I make exceptions for them.

This is just one of the many problems that are most effectively dealt with by using the "stuck-record" technique.

For example, you could say, "I understand your frustration, but I can't make exceptions for anyone." Or, "I'd like to make an exception in this case, but I can't." If the person continues to complain, calmly repeat exactly what you said before. Repeat it again if the person continues to badger you. Don't raise your voice or get defensive. You'll find that the third time you make the comment, the client will hear you. But remember: when you can't do what a person wants, try to offer at least two alternative solutions if at all possible.

Using the Telephone

If you're like me, when you run into someone who doesn't answer the phone properly your impression of the whole company goes rapidly downhill. Remember, if you answer the phone incorrectly, you're likely to "turn off" potential and even regular customers.

Creating a favorable impression for your firm is imperative. You may be the first and in some cases the only contact the customer or client has with your firm. Here are some suggestions:

Telephone etiquette
1. Answer calls promptly—on the first ring if possible.
2. Transfer calls effectively. (See "Telephone Responses.")
3. Give progress reports to callers if they're on hold.
4. Never put your hand over the mouthpiece. (The client will think you're being sneaky or that you're talking about them.)
5. No matter how you're feeling at that moment, don't pass your bad mood on to your customer.
6. Keep your cool with difficult customers.
7. *Apologize if you've made a mistake.*
8. Try to give that little extra service to customers that they'll remember for the future.
9. Learn the correct way of making and logging long-distance phone calls.
10. Learn the techniques of feedback and paraphrasing so messages aren't misunderstood.
11. When taking a name, ask the person to spell it for you. Then in brackets, add a phonetic spelling of the name so you won't mispronounce it later.
12. If you leave your work station, make sure you let the receptionist know, or have someone else answer your phone.
13. Keep paper and pen next to *every* telephone.
14. If you must leave the phone to get information, ask whether the caller will wait or will let you call him or her back.
15. If callers ask for information you can't provide, tell them you'll get back to them with the answer. Either return the call yourself, or have someone do it who's more familiar with the subject than you. But make sure someone follows up. The latter suggestion may be preferable when the person may have additional questions during the conversation that you wouldn't be able to answer.
16. Use the caller's name whenever practical (don't overdo this though). Practice the correct pronunciation of the name.

17. Place long-distance calls yourself. Having your secretary do this often wastes the client's time. This suggests to people that you think their time is less valuable than yours.
18. Have notes ready, related to the call being made, so you won't forget important details. If the call has to be returned, these notes will help you remember everything you wished to discuss.
19. Identify yourself when you answer the phone: e.g., "Bill Baker, Shipping Department."

Remember, you want to be both polite and pleasant; you want the caller to feel important; you want to avoid wasting the caller's time and the company's time. And above all you want to help the caller achieve the purpose of the call.

With a few standard responses you can meet all these goals in most of the situations you will encounter. A number of these standard responses are outlined below.

Telephone responses

Situation	*Response*
Answering an incoming call.	Accounting Department, Bill Jones speaking.
The person called is on another line.	Ms. Jones is talking on another line. Would you like to hold, or may I ask her to call you?
The person called is away from his or her desk for a few minutes.	Mr. Jones is not in his office right now. May I take a message?
The caller reached the wrong extension.	Our accounting department handles that type of information. May I transfer you?
The person called is in a meeting until 3:00 p.m.	Ms. Jones is attending a meeting until 3:00 p.m. May I ask her to call you?
The person called is with a client.	Mr. Jones is with a client. May I ask him to call you?
The person called has left the office for the afternoon.	Ms. Jones won't be back this afternoon. Would you like her to call you tomorrow?

You need to know who is calling.	May I tell Mr. Jones who's calling please?
The person called is not in yet.	Ms. Jones is not in the office just now. May I ask her to call you? NOTE: Avoid saying, "She hasn't come in yet today," which makes it appear as if she slept in.
The person called is ill.	Mr. Jones isn't in today. May I ask him to call you, or could someone else help you?
You need to give the caller a progress report.	Ms. Jones is still on his line. May I take a message, or ask her to call you?
You are returning to a call on hold.	Thank you for waiting.
The person called is out of town.	Mr. Jones is out of the office until June fourth. May I take a message, or could someone else help you? NOTE: Avoid saying, "He's out of town," which could tell burglars it's safe to break into his home.
You are answering a call transferred to you.	Accounting Department, Bill Jones speaking. May I help you?
The person called is out of the office but will be returning.	Ms. Jones is away from the office until 2:00 p.m. May I have her call you when she returns? NOTE: Avoid saying, "I have no idea where she is!" (This sounds very unprofessional. You should know where she is!)
The person called is out for coffee.	I expect Mr. Jones in about twenty minutes. May I ask him to call you?
The person called is out for lunch.	I expect Ms. Jones at about 1:00 p.m. May I ask her to call you? NOTE: Don't say she's "Out to lunch," which could mean to some people that she's missing brainpower.

The person called is busy and doesn't want to be disturbed.	Mr. Jones isn't available until 3:00 p.m. Could someone else help you, or may I take a message and have him return your call? NOTE: Saying, "He's tied up right now," brings forth images of someone being tied up with ropes.
You are completing a phone call.	Thank you for calling. Goodbye.
You are placing a call.	Good morning. This is Bill Jones of the XYZ Company calling. May I speak with Mr. Smith, please?

Never give replies like, "She left for lunch about half an hour ago. Call back in two hours, she'll probably be back by then." Or, "Today's Thursday and she seldom gets in before 10:30 on Thursday." Such replies create a poor impression of the person called and, ultimately, of the company as well.

One answer that covers a multitude of situations is, "I'm sorry, Mr. Jones isn't available right now." Mr. Jones might be sitting right beside you, but he's "not available" to the caller. This makes it unnecessary for receptionists and secretaries to lie for their supervisors. Use this when your supervisor wants you to say, untruthfully, that he or she is not in the office.

Using Common Sense and Good Manners

Here are some situations where good old "common sense" should prevail:

1. Your supervisor has tackled a mountain of work and has left word you're not to disturb him unless the building's on fire. The president of your company phones and asks to speak to your supervisor.
There are exceptions to every rule. This is obviously one of them.

2. You always seem to receive wrong-number phone calls for another firm with a similar phone number.
Don't waste time feeling angry. Instead, look up the number of the company and be ready to give the right number to the caller.

3. Your municipal government department is similar to another department in the federal government. People seem to think you're able to answer their questions.

Have a set spiel explaining the differences in your functions and give callers the correct number. Don't lose your cool—they're not trying to annoy you.

4. You have to escort a visitor from the reception area to your supervisor's office. Do you:
   a. precede the visitor, stating, "Will you follow me, please"?
   b. let the visitor go first, stating, "It's down this corridor, first door on your right"?

The correct answer is a.

5. You bring a visitor to your supervisor's office. They've never met before. Do you:
   a. let the visitor walk in?
   b. announce the visitor, saying, "(Supervisor's name), this is Mr. Jones from XYZ Company"?
   c. introduce each to the other?

The correct answer is b.

6. Your supervisor calls you into her office while she has a male visitor. The visitor stands when you enter. Should you:
   a. nod at the visitor, and sit down?
   b. nod at the visitor, and say, "Won't you please be seated?"?
   c. Say, "Hello," and sit down?

Both a and c are correct.

7. Your supervisor's spouse drops in just before closing time. Should you:
   a. call your supervisor on the intercom and follow the instructions given?
   b. offer the visitor a chair in the reception area?
   c. smile and make small talk until your supervisor is available?

The correct answer is a, unless your supervisor is unavailable for a while, then b is correct.

SPECIAL SITUATIONS

Government Offices

Government workers face special problems with clients. Because governments are not in competition with other firms, the client does not have the option of going elsewhere. As a result, people often go into a government office with a ready-made chip on their shoulder.

Another problem that government workers face is the attitude, "You're working for me. Give me service, or else!" Government employees need to accept that this attitude is common and quite understandable.

These two problems mean that government workers need more empathy and interpersonal skills than other types of employees. Government employers should keep this in mind when hiring staff who deal with the public.

Doctors' Offices

"I work in a doctor's office, and people often call up and want an appointment that day. If I'm booked up, but suggest 10:00 a.m. the next morning, I run into arguments. How can I placate these people and feel less guilty about not being able to help them sooner?"

One reply could be, "I'm sorry Dr. Greg can't see you today. However, I have two vacancies tomorrow morning. Would you prefer a 10:00 a.m. or an 11:30 a.m. appointment?"

Absolve yourself of any guilt this problem generates. If you're doing your job the best way you can, there's no need for you to accept guilty feelings. In the initial situation, when you couldn't conform to the patients' wishes, they likely felt that they had lost control. Giving alternatives will help them regain the feeling that they are in control.

"I'm a receptionist in a doctor's office. Last week, a woman came in with her rowdy two-year-old son. He proceeded to get into everything

in the office. I finally picked him up and plunked him on his mother's knee, saying, 'Does this child belong to you? He's getting into things, so you'll have to watch him.' Five minutes later, it was her turn to see the doctor, and she had the nerve to say, 'Look after Johnnie.' I let her know that it wasn't my job to babysit her child. She should have brought someone else to babysit him. I was too busy. She eventually took Johnnie in with her, but she wasn't happy. How could I have handled that situation better?"

This problem occurs in doctors', dentists' and lawyers' offices and it's a serious one. Never pick up children or restrain them unless they're in danger of injuring themselves or others. If you do, the mother could charge you with assault!

Bring the child's disruptive behavior to the attention of the mother. If the behavior persists, ask the mother and child to leave. You shouldn't have to babysit, unless there's an emergency of some sort. Keep in mind that, if you agree to care for the child, you may be legally liable should the child be injured while in your care. Check the laws in your area and inform your supervisor of your obligation and liability should you be asked to do this as part of your duties.

Some offices have had to post signs such as: "Your children's behavior is your responsibility. If they're misbehaving or causing a disturbance, they'll be asked to leave."

Many medical offices have toys for children to play with, but many have signs stating, "These toys are for patients' use only." This discourages parents from using the staff as a babysitter for children who are not there to see the doctor. Again, let your supervisor be your guide on what rules and regulations apply.

"I work in a doctor's office, and callers often refuse to tell me the reason for their appointment. I explain that I need to know so I know how much time to book them for. Their standard answer seems to be, 'I only need to see him for five minutes.' I then book them in for ten minutes, and find that they need fifteen or twenty because of the complexity of their ailment. If they had explained their ailment to me, I would have known from past patients that they would need that long. Why do patients do this? Do they think I'm being nosy?"

Understand that they may have what they consider a private problem to discuss with the doctor. They may feel that you have no right to know about their innermost secrets. Try using empathy: "I know the matter is personal, but you haven't given me the information I need to set up an appointment." Let them know that you're following the doctor's orders. Use the "stuck-record" method if necessary. Or suggest an alternative, such as, "Would you rather Dr. Smith called you about this matter?"

Restaurants and Hotels

"I work in a restaurant as a hostess. I had a situation the other day that I didn't handle well. There was only one table for two left. First in line was a woman with her son. She explained that it was his birthday, a special occasion for them. They didn't have reservations.

"I was ready to seat them after stating that it was the last table left, when the couple behind her spoke up. 'We have reservations for 7:00. It is now 7:00, and I understand that you have only one table left. My wife and I have to be at a movie at 8:15, so we can't wait until another table's available. We want that one!' They pointed to the last table.

"The woman and the couple argued about who should get the table, and I finally seated the couple with the reservation. The woman and her son became upset and soon left the restaurant before a table was available."

There are some situations where "you're damned if you do, and you're damned if you don't." This is one of those situations. Because of the scarcity of tables available, you should have interviewed everyone waiting, to see if there were any who had reservations. The woman and her son would have had to wait for another table. You chose the right solution.

"I'm the registration clerk at a hotel. At 5:00 p.m., a woman came in to register for her room. The hotel was still full from a convention. People were late checking out, so her room wasn't ready. She started running down the hotel, stating what a miserable day she'd been having. The only thing I could suggest was a hospitality suite until hers was ready.

She wasn't very happy, but accepted it anyway. What else could I have suggested?"

Find out what extras your hotel offers should this happen in the future. You could have tried the approach of offering alternatives, for instance: "Would you accept the hospitality suite until your room is ready? Or would you rather leave your bags with me and enjoy a complimentary beverage and meal in our restaurant?" (Remember that at 5:00 p.m. she might appreciate refreshments or a meal.) Psychologically this approach puts her back in control because she can choose what she wants to do.

Whenever your company or one of its representatives has caused grief to a client, the client deserves tender, loving care to correct the problem. This T.L.C. can be as simple as solving the problem, or as elaborate as a cash or merchandise bonus. Hotels often give complimentary baskets of fruit or better accommodation if they've caused a client difficulty.

What extras could your company offer to avoid losing the future business of clients who have a legitimate beef?

"I'm a hostess in the banquet room. I was responsible for the comfort and service guests received at a function in the banquet room. The air conditioning wasn't working properly, so we posted NO SMOKING *signs throughout the room. The meeting was just going to start when I spotted a man lighting up. I explained about the air conditioning, and asked him to put out his cigarette. He started a disturbance, shouting, 'Discrimination.' I ended up having to call the manager to get him to put it out. What should I have done?"*

This man has all the attributes of a "Class Clown." He couldn't help but see the signs, so he knew he was breaking the rules when he lit up. You should have been ready for trouble. I would have told the man that I would like to speak to him outside the room (which removes him from the audience). Then I would have explained the reasons for the NO SMOKING signs.

If he protested, I would have tried the stuck-record technique or given him alternatives. If he wished to smoke, he could do so in the hallway, or in the cafeteria, but not in the banquet room. If he persisted after that point, I would have involved the manager or security officer.

Recreational Facilities

"I work for a recreational facility. I spend most of my day giving people information about public swimming times or ice time. I find this very boring. I also have much more pressing duties to attend to."

Certainly it's not very stimulating giving out the same information over and over again, but have you checked your job description? I bet you'll find that this is the prime function of your position. Repeat calls may be unavoidable, because schedules of recreational facilities change so often. To cut down on many repeat calls, ask clients if they would like to come in and pick up a schedule or offer to mail them one. If you still can't reconcile yourself to this part of your responsibilities, you may have to consider whether you're in the wrong job or are overqualified for the position.

Services to the Elderly

"I have to deal with elderly people. What are some of the things I should remember when dealing with them?"

Sometimes elderly clients can be difficult to deal with. A lot of things are happening to them. Quite often their health isn't as good as it used to be. It's possible their hearing isn't good, or that their thought processes have slowed down a bit.

But imagine how annoying it is to a sprightly eighty-year-old to be yelled at because the speaker assumes all elderly people are deaf. Those who can't hear properly normally have a hearing aid. Don't automatically raise your voice just because a person has white hair.

Again, elderly people may not appreciate being treated as though they're a little simple. Avoid talking down to them. If you're not sure that they have understood, encourage them to paraphrase for you, so you can be sure you have made yourself clear.

Clients with Disabilities

"I sometimes encounter a client who stutters. How should I deal with that problem?"

What errors do you think you commit when in conversation with someone who stutters? Do you finish the sentence for that person? If you finish the sentence incorrectly, this forces the stutterer to start at the beginning again. Can you imagine the double annoyance this is for the person? Stutterers often feel anxiety about being misunderstood. You double their anxiety when you misinterpret what they're going to say by finishing their sentence for them. Have a heart!

Here are a few things to keep in mind when conversing with someone who stutters. Most stutterers are of average or high intelligence. Their brains simply go too fast for their mouths to say what they want to say. Often when they were children, parents and teachers made them self-conscious about their speech, which makes the problem worse.

Start off by letting the stutterer know that you're willing to listen. You do this by using good listening techniques. Give comfortable eye contact, nod your head, ask questions, and by all means let the person finish what he or she is saying. Try to give the impression that you have time for them to say what they want to say. If they try to rush what they're saying, it'll just take longer because of their nervousness.

"I find it difficult dealing with clients who are handicapped. I realize that this is my problem, but what can I do to overcome it?"

The biggest beef handicapped people have against others is that they're treated as nonentities. Do you talk to the companion of the person in the wheelchair, instead of the person in the chair? Many in wheelchairs aren't even given eye contact—in fact most people do anything but give them eye contact. This makes them feel non-existent, and they respond with hostility.

Next time you see someone in a wheelchair, nod or smile and make eye contact. It's better for all concerned if you treat the disabled like everyone else and with respect. Even a severely mentally handicapped person appreciates this.

Offer to help if the person appears to need it. If your offer is rebuffed with a curt, "I can do it myself," don't feel guilty because of the comment. Offer to help, because it may be needed, but respect the person's desire to assert his or her independence and self-sufficiency.

OTHER TYPES OF PROBLEMS

The Client Has Already Had the Run-Around

You answer the phone for your company. The person on the phone is really upset. She has had the proverbial run-around. She says, "You're the fourth person I've spoken to without getting any answers. Can't anyone help me?"

This person has been the victim of the pass-the-buck syndrome, and the buck should stop with you. Saying "Sorry, this is the wrong department" isn't going to be acceptable. She wants her problem solved, and she sees you as being able to help her. She doesn't care if it's "your department" or not. She was frustrated when she first called, but she's now well on her way to becoming unglued. If you also lose your cool and become angry, the problem will get even worse.

Out-of-control anger can be compared to "temporary insanity." If possible, try to prevent your client from becoming temporarily insane, or bring her back to sanity if she's already there. You do this by starting the problem on its way to being solved. If you can do *anything* to move toward a solution, the client will appreciate your help.

This could be done by obtaining all the pertinent information necessary to get the person helped. Then ask for the person's telephone number and have the appropriate employee call her back *within a reasonable length of time*! If the employee can't respond right away, keep the client informed. Give the client your name and number so she can call you back if she doesn't obtain satisfaction from your reference person. Then and only then are you off the hook with the client.

The Client Acts the "Class Clown"

"Class clowns" are difficult to handle. In school, they're the ones who disrupt the class and keep things in an uproar. The aim of this behavior is to get attention. Children who are class clowns crave any attention they can get and are perfectly willing to accept negative attention rather than have none at all.

How do experienced teachers handle this kind of child? They give the child the attention he or she craves—but for *good* behavior. When the child misbehaves, he or she is isolated from the rest of the class (the opposite of what the child wants). Usually the teacher will take the child away from the group and quietly speak to the offender.

When these children become adults, their "class clown" behavior often continues. They're the people who make sure everyone in the room knows how annoyed they are at something your company has done. They're the ones who want *immediate* attention. If they don't get it, they become verbally abusive and upset everyone around them.

How do you handle these people? The same way you treat children who exhibit this kind of negative behavior. Take them aside, preferably into a private office. (Don't attempt this if they look physically abusive.) Explain to them that you'll be happy to handle their problem as soon as it's their turn, that if they continue their unacceptable behavior you'll be forced to ignore them. Then return them to the area where they were waiting and handle the next customer.

Obviously, before you attempt the above, you should have your supervisor's full approval. If you don't, you may find yourself in the middle if the client decides to go higher with the problem. If you regularly have behavior problems to deal with, discuss tactics with your supervisor. Review possible strategies and obtain your supervisor's suggestions on how to handle problems. Both of you will then know that difficult situations will be handled consistently.

The Client Refuses to Deal with a Woman

Sally Brown, who's the credit manager for a large construction firm, solved a problem she was facing in a rather humorous way. She had to put up with what seemed like too many clients who insisted on "talking to a man." She solved the problem by patching the calls through to Sam, the janitor in the building. Sam had been clued in and knew how to handle that kind of call. His standard reply was, "I don't know why you're talking to me. Sally Brown's our credit manager. I'll transfer you back to her, and she can look after you."

Another solution would be for Sally to answer her phone by identifying herself clearly. She should say, "Sally Brown, Credit Manager, may I help you?" Most people assume that you're in a low-level position if you answer your phone by just your first name. Most men answer with full name and title. Women should do the same in order to receive the respect they deserve.

The Client Blames You for Someone Else's Mistake

"I had a problem last week that reduced me to tears. I'm the stockroom clerk in the warehouse of our company. I haven't been on the job for long, and the warehouse manager left me in charge while he picked up some equipment. An angry client phoned in to complain that we had delivered the wrong part and it was costing his company a mint. He called me stupid and acted as if it was all my fault!

"He had ordered the part two months before I even started with the company! I kept insisting that he would have to phone back in fifteen minutes when the warehouse manager returned. I used the "stuck-record" technique, but it didn't seem to work. How should I have handled this irate customer?"

In this case, I can see why the "stuck-record" technique didn't work. You forgot to "turn off" your defense mechanism when the client started yelling at you. What you could have done was take down information as soon as the person started talking. You would have paraphrased and asked questions that would have assisted in solving his problem.

As it was, when the warehouse manager returned fifteen minutes later, no one had started to solve the person's problem. It's likely the manager had to deal with an even angrier client fifteen minutes later! If you had obtained the pertinent information, the warehouse manager would have had some answers for the irate client when he returned his call. Remember this whenever taking a "beef call" for another.

The Client Drops in Without an Appointment

"How should I handle regular clients who just drop in, expecting someone to see them?"

Using the stuck-record technique, tell them, "I'm sorry, you can't see Mr. Jones without an appointment. Would you like to make one for another time?" If the client objects, say "My instructions are that no one's seen unless he or she has an appointment. Would you like to make an appointment for another time?"

The Client Is Long-Winded

"I handle a busy switchboard. When callers want to give me their life story, how can I handle them tactfully?"

Sometimes, it's necessary to interrupt them (they do have to come up for air). Ask if they can *briefly* explain the problem as you'll be passing them on to another person.

"I have a client whom I can't keep on track. He's always going off topic."

When dealing with a compulsive talker, use every conversational gap to guide the conversation toward accomplishing the needs of the phone call. Never show your boredom or frustration, as it'll offend the client. If you give alternatives, the client has to make some decisions. Summarize your conversation, stating what you'll be doing for them, or what they'll be doing for you. Then use this closing clincher: "I believe we've covered everything. I won't take up any more of your valuable time."

The Client Needs an Immediate Answer

"I work in a by-law office, and people phoning in need information imme-diately. I can't contact the by-law officer because he's out of the office."

One solution is to have a beeper for the by-law officer. Another is to have the officer phone in on a regular basis to obtain messages. Use feedback with the by-law officer to explain the problems you're having with clients and ask his or her assistance in finding solutions.

The Client Is a Know-It-All

"I have trouble dealing with 'know-it-all' people who ask you for infor-mation, but really just want to give their own version of what's right."

First—listen to the client's ideas and ask for any facts that support those views. Then, using the information available to you, tell the client the real facts. Refer to rules, regulations, policies and procedure manuals or other written data if necessary.

The Client Is Condescending or Rude

"How do I deal with people who are condescending to me—treat me like dirt? They give me the impression that because I'm a clerk I don't know anything. They usually come in to get information regarding col-lege courses."

These are people who probably lack self-assurance and try to put you down to make themselves feel more important. They may or may not use sarcasm to do this. Turn off your defense mechanism. Realize that you are in control of the situation. After all, *they* are coming to *you* for infor-mation. Just give them the information they request. Don't allow them to make you lose your cool. You might ask them the show-stopping question, "What do you want me to do to solve this problem?" This often stops them long enough to clarify that they really want from you.

"I've a client who's very rude to me every time he calls in, but is as 'sweet as pie' to my boss. How can I get this person to treat me better?"

Using feedback and the expression "I have a problem, and I need your help in solving it . . . ," explain to your supervisor the rudeness of this client. Ask your supervisor to speak to this person about the matter. The client should know that this is unacceptable behavior to any employee of the company. If your supervisor won't back you up, transfer this person's call directly to the supervisor without having any further exchange with that person.

The Client Puts Your Long-Distance Call on Hold

"When I call long distance, I get furious if the receptionist puts me on hold without asking whether I object. How can I deal with being put on 'ignore' in the future?"

If this is a regular occurrence, talk to the receptionist's supervisor and explain the inconvenience and costs this delay gives you. I jump right in and say that my call is long-distance even before identifying whom I am calling. I say, "Long distance for Marie Baker." They assume I'm a long-distance operator and put the call through right away. A more drastic solution is to bill this client for the time you were put on hold.

You Have to Deal with Two Clients Simultaneously

"I never know whether I should handle the person on the phone or the person who has waited to see me for fifteen minutes. Who should get priority?"

Answer the phone and tell the caller you're with a client and will be a few minutes. Give alternatives. Ask whether the caller would like to call back, have you return the call later or be put on hold. Then alternate between those who have come in in person and those who phone in.

"I work for a parts department of an auto-supply firm. I'm trying to get them to set up a numbering system, so customers are dealt with in turn. Right now, because it's hard to keep track of who is next (I have to go into the warehouse to get their parts) I often can't be sure in what order to help people. I've had to referee several battles about whose turn it is, and I find that it gets me rattled."

After you decided whom you would serve first and had eventually dealt with the two irate customers, you should have reminded yourself, "That was certainly an unpleasant encounter, but I did the best I could." Remember, in situations like this, no matter whom you serve first, you're "damned if you do and damned if you don't." You have no reason to take on guilt feelings because you couldn't please them both simultaneously. Use feedback with your supervisor to explain the difficulties not having a numbering system is causing you and the rest of the staff. (You could also try setting up an informal numbering system on your own, while you wait for the firm to act.)

The Client Refuses to Wait His or Her Turn

"My boss, a lawyer, is very busy. Last week a friend of his needed some legal advice and expected service immediately. I explained the situation and suggested that he make an appointment. The friend barged right past me into my boss's office, where he was in a meeting with a client. How could I have handled that situation better?"

Talk to your supervisor and ask him what you should do if a similar situation happens in the future. Unless you had used some fast judo or karate, the friend would have been in your supervisor's office before you could react anyway. Throw your guilt trip out the window. At the time you did the best you could to handle the situation.

The Client Uses Profane Language or Threatening Behavior

"What should I do when my caller uses profane language on the phone? Do I have to put up with that kind of garbage?"

I don't believe anyone should have to put up with profane language. You should be able to hang up on the caller. Check with your supervisor to see what you're expected to do. It's possible, because of the work you do, that you do have to put up with that kind of garbage—for instance, if you're working in an emergency ward of a hospital. It's part of the pattern for some people to start swearing when upset about something. You can't just refuse to handle the problem of this upset person. If you're working on a crisis or emergency line of any kind, you have to know that this language may go with the territory. You may, however, ask such callers to clean up their language so you can handle their difficulty better. But above all, make sure you know what your supervisor wants you to do.

"How about drunk or threatening people?"

Another topic that you must talk about to your supervisor *before* it happens. Know when to call in a security guard or the police. Knowing what steps to take and having an emergency plan of your own makes you more confident when having to deal with such unexpected and unsettling problems.

5

DEALING WITH DIFFICULT SUPERVISORS

If you're not enjoying your work, there could be a number of reasons why. One possible cause of job dissatisfaction is poor supervision. Some individuals have been chosen for their supervisory positions because they know a lot about the type of work done by those they are supervising. They may know next to nothing, however, about how to motivate *people*.

If you think your supervisor's "style" of managing is responsible for your job dissatisfaction, this chapter is for you.

POOR MOTIVATORS

Many employees are self-motivating and will work well even under poor supervision. Every employee, however, can respond to and benefit from a supervisor who understands what motivates people to do their best work. Because not every employee is the same, a good supervisor will develop insight into which employees respond best to praise, which to monetary incentives and which to opportunities to learn new things or to prepare for promotion.

If your motivation at work is suffering, it may be because your supervisor doesn't understand that some or all of the following working conditions can have a powerfully *de*motivating effect.

1. ***Restrictive supervision.*** You'll likely obtain less job satisfaction if your supervisor gives you little chance to take an active part in how you complete your assignments. The more employees participate in how they do things, the more cooperative they will be.

   Supervisors who use an authoritarian leadership style are setting themselves up to fail. If you have this type of supervisor, try feedback to alleviate the problem. If your supervisor won't be reasonable and you can't change his or her behavior, you may have to suffer for a while until a promotion is available. Alternatively, you could take a lateral move to another department or, as a last resort, leave the company you're with.

2. ***Lack of recognition.*** Supervisors demotivate staff if they identify only what their subordinates have done wrong. They should concentrate instead on what they have done right, to encourage better performance.

   In the old school of management, supervisors believed it was their right to take credit for new ideas suggested by their subordinates. As you might expect, this just demotivates employees, discourages new ideas and perpetuates mediocre performance and marginal productivity. Progressive supervisors are learning that if they give employees credit where credit is due, their staff is motivated to perform better. Employees whose supervisors are still stingy with recognition could try using feedback to alleviate this problem. Possibly, the supervisor isn't aware of how demotivating his or her actions are. Say, "I have a problem, and I need your help in solving it. In the past week I've gone out of my way to do an exceptional job on the Miller project and have worked overtime to meet the deadline. I'm discouraged because all I've heard about the project is the 2 percent I did wrong. What about the 98 percent I did right? It's not very encouraging to hear only the negatives. Do you understand what I mean?"

   This should help the supervisor do a better job in future by giving positive reinforcement when it's due.

3. ***Monotonous work.*** Companies implement job rotation for their employees in an attempt to make employees' jobs more interesting. Job rotation is possible if there are several employees in a company who work at substantially the same class or level of work and in the

same pay range. Employers and employees alike benefit from job rotation, because staff members can fill more than one job and the work of absent employees can be done by someone else. If your company is doing this, management is trying to keep your work interesting. If they haven't tried job rotation, suggest they do so, for all your sakes!

4. ***Little opportunity to try new ideas.*** Employee motivation also suffers when supervisors ignore workers' suggestions for better ways of doing their jobs. Because the employees are doing the actual work, they are often in the best position to come up with better and quicker ways to do the job.

   If your supervisor is weak in this area, plant seeds for change slowly. Let him or her get used to a new idea gradually. Use facts to back up your suggestions, and identify any cost reduction that can be achieved by doing it the new way. Be open, however, to legitimate reasons why your idea won't work. If your supervisor won't respond to any suggestions, use feedback to describe your frustration.

5. ***No opportunities to acquire new skills.*** At one time, companies spent many training dollars on their employees and still couldn't keep up with the demand for competent qualified people. Recently, companies have had to tighten their training budgets. Companies may refuse to give training that they believe employees can't use right away. Employees whose promotions are six months to one year away may find it difficult to obtain training.

   To be sure they are ready for the next step up, employees who find themselves in this position would be wise to obtain and pay for this training themselves. The employee thus gains an edge over others who have not acquired the necessary skills. Dollars spent on training are a good investment by the employee.

6. ***Absence of job descriptions and performance appraisals.*** Companies that practice good management systems know that both accurate, up-to-date job descriptions and performance appraisals are essential for high productivity and motivation of staff. When staff know what's expected of them, they perform better.

If more than 10 percent of your duties fit into the category "other duties as assigned," your job description isn't accurate. How do you go about getting a more realistic one? If your company is using an official classification system, they know that no more than 10 percent is allowed under that category. In that case, you could simply itemize your duties and the percentage of your time spent on each item. Your request for reclassification will be based on factual information. Or, if your job description is more than two years old, it's probably outdated. Again, you need to itemize your duties and the percentage of your time each takes, before pointing out discrepancies between your job description and your actual job and asking for reclassification. A good time to ask for a job-description update is when you have your yearly performance appraisal.

What if tasks are regularly added to your duties without any reclassification of your position? If you are always being given more of the *same* kind of task (job dumping), you can't request a reclassification. But if your new tasks have a different level of responsibility, then your job probably should be reclassified. You would need to use facts to prove that your responsibility level had changed.

In large companies, there are usually formal classification systems. If you work for a small company, you might have some difficulty. Job classification is based on the responsibility level of the tasks performed by the person in the position. If the level of responsibility changes, either upward or downward, the position is usually reclassified. For example, a secretary whose supervisor takes on extra responsibilities will most likely need a job reclassification, because the responsibility level of the secretary rises with the supervisor's. On the other hand, if the supervisor's position is abolished, and the secretary now works for four lower-level people, the responsibility level of the job will be lower, and the position could be reclassified to a lower level.

What if your employer says, "We don't have job descriptions here"? In that case, you should write one yourself (using examples found at the library, or accurate descriptions of a friend's position as a guideline). Take it to your supervisor and ask for approval. If approval is refused, ask, "How can I do a good job for you, if neither of us knows what I'm supposed to do?"

7. ***Discrepancy between pay and level of responsibility.*** If you're convinced that your salary level is too low for the kind of work you're doing, you'll have to look at your current job description, make any changes necessary, then ask for an appointment with your supervisor. At the meeting, explain that your duties are listed incorrectly and that you have much more responsibility than the description shows. Or perhaps your job description is accurate, but the salary range for it doesn't reflect the job's importance to the company. Find out what similar positions are earning in competitive companies. Expressions such as "I think I'm underpaid" will not help you; go in equipped with *facts*. You must be able to give reasons to back up your request for more money. If this fails, you may have to leave the company you're with and look elsewhere.

8. ***Unpaid overtime.*** In some areas, an employer has the choice of either paying employees time and a half for overtime or giving them time off in lieu of overtime pay. Employees must sign an agreement for the latter option to be valid. The law in some regions states that overtime pay should be awarded for any time worked over eight hours a day, or forty-four hours a week.

   If you don't know the labor laws of your area, it's up to you to find out.

WORKPLACE BULLYING

Many people who are guilty of workplace bullying are in positions of power and were most likely bullies at school. Workplace bullying (harassment or assault) may consist of a single traumatic incident or several incidents. It may also follow a pattern of constant fault-finding, criticizing, segregating, excluding, undermining, over weeks or months.

Society makes the assumption that bullies are male, but women can be as vicious as men. Workplace bullies often appear competent and professional at their jobs, but behind the façade, they're inadequate and inept. Some have unpredictable mood swings—they're like time bombs. They

gain gratification from provoking people into emotional or irrational responses. The vulnerability of others is the primary stimulant to bullies.
Bullying includes:

- belittling, demeaning or patronizing the victim—especially in front of others;
- shouting at and threatening the target, often in front of others;
- making snide comments to see if the person will fight back;
- finding fault and criticizing everything the victim says and does, or twisting, distorting and misrepresenting the victim. The criticism may be of a trivial nature; often there's a grain of truth in it, which can dupe the victim into believing the criticism is valid.
- stubbornly refusing to recognize the victim's contributions;
- attempting to chip away at the target's status, self-confidence, worth and potential;
- treating the victim differently—showing favoritism to others and bias toward the victim.

Many bullies have:

- greater-than-average aggressive behavior patterns;
- a desire to dominate peers;
- a need to feel in control, to win;
- no sense of remorse for hurting another;
- an inability to accept responsibility for their behavior.

Who Are the Targets of Bullying?

Targets of bullying are assumed to be loners, but most are independent, self-reliant people who have no need for gangs or cliques, have no need to impress, and are not interested in office politics. Bullies select individuals who prefer to use dialogue to resolve conflict, who have a low propensity for violence, and who will go to great lengths to avoid conflict. They constantly try to use negotiation rather than resort to grievance and legal action. Targets are chosen because they're competent and popular. Bullies are jealous of the easy and stable relationships that targets have with others.

How to Deal with Workplace Bullying

Every company should have clearly defined policies and procedures relating to workplace bullying. Review them and follow the procedures. If your company does not, search online or consult a lawyer, ideally one involved with labor or human rights, for information regarding the appropriate government agency to contact.

THE AGGRESSIVE SUPERVISOR

In an ideal world all supervisors would be assertive (rather than passive or aggressive), pleasant, supportive, efficient, tactful and blessed with superior insight into human nature. In the real world, however, supervisors display the usual range of human faults and failings. Supervisors who use aggressive behavior to dominate and control their staff are among the most difficult for an employee to deal with.

Aggressive supervisors haven't learned one of the fundamentals of good supervision. Employees can't be forced into doing a good job, they're led into it. Supervisors are bound to receive poor productivity from their staff if they:

- discipline employees publicly;
- bully them into working excessively long hours;
- are hypercritical and impossible to please;
- criticize individuals rather than behavior.

Before you decide to say anything to an aggressive supervisor, ask yourself if you might make matters worse by saying something. If this person treats *everyone* the same belligerent way, it may not be worth the risk of discussing the matter. You may have to mark time until you can get away from this bully.

If you decide it might help to discuss the problem, use feedback to let your supervisor know how his or her behavior is affecting you. This takes courage, but at least you will know you made an effort to improve matters. Talk to your supervisor privately about his or her aggressive behavior. If the problem is "labeling," for example, say, "I have a problem and I need your help in solving it. I find it difficult to handle the put-downs you've been giving me lately. I can't defend my actions when you call me names. The way it is now, I don't know how to improve my performance or what you really want of me. Could you give me examples of why you think I'm ignorant?"

If the situation doesn't change, don't go higher up to his or her supervisor to complain. Instead:

- put up with it as long as you can, then ask for a transfer to another position in the company;
- talk to someone in your personnel department; or
- leave for greener pastures elsewhere.

Go higher up the chain of command only when the supervisor's behavior is affecting the rest of the staff. Only group complaints can oust a bad supervisor and then only if the complaint is handled correctly. Make sure the group uses facts to explain its grievances. Have details of what has actually happened, costs in dollars, damage to customer relations, delays, unmet deadlines, unnecessary overtime, production stoppages, etc.

When you feel your supervisor has removed all the pride and pleasure you obtain from your work, then it's time to leave.

As we have seen, aggressive behavior can take a variety of forms. Ways of dealing with some of these are worth discussing in detail.

1. ***Sarcasm.*** Some sarcasm is nothing more than harmless kidding. It is non-threatening and can be fun. However, sarcasm can also be hurtful, designed to make others feel small. People using it feel a sense of power at seeing other people squirm. Hurtful sarcasm is a form of indirect aggression—one of the sneakiest, most manipulative and underhanded methods of getting your way.

   People who use hurtful sarcasm often don't feel very good about themselves, so they attempt to put others down to make themselves feel more important. The game continues when others respond defensively or act hurt. Sarcastic people want others to get angry and defend themselves. Remind yourself not to respond negatively to their remarks. Try to stick to the facts.

Think for a minute: who's in control in the situation when sarcasm is used? You are (the recipient of the sarcasm) until you reply. Should you respond to sarcasm with more sarcasm? No—if you do, you often just encourage more of the same. Instead, try to analyze why the person might feel the need to put you down. Once you have an idea of what really prompts the sarcasm, you'll be able to deal with the actual issue.

Don't react to sarcasm—turn it off. The sarcastic person won't know what to do, because you're not playing by "the rules." When it's no longer fun to throw things at you, the culprit will take his or her sarcastic remarks elsewhere.

If you can't stay quiet, and you feel that the sarcasm warrants a response, you might say, "Your last comment was very sarcastic, and a put-down. Put-downs hurt. Can you explain why you said what you did?" Or, "Why do you feel you have to give me a put-down like that?" Or, "That was pretty sarcastic. What is it that you really want to say to me that you're covering up with sarcasm?" Make aggressive people account for their actions. Often they aren't aware of how destructive their behavior is to others.

When I was doing the research for my first book, *Escaping the Pink-Collar Ghetto*, I interviewed more than 700 managers (695 of them men) to see why they weren't promoting more women. Initially, I was met with a crossed-arms defensive stance from most of the managers. I knew they were on the defensive when the sarcasm started to flow. My instinctive reaction was to fight sarcasm with sarcasm but instead, I stood back from the situation and tried to analyze it. I concluded that these managers felt that when I asked, "Why aren't you promoting more women?" I was accusing them of discriminatory behavior.

I reassured them by explaining fully what I was there to accomplish: that I really needed their input to find out what mistakes women were making that kept them from being promoted. I gave several examples other companies had given me and asked them if the same was true in their company as well. Soon they realized that I was there only to obtain information and their help, not to push them into defending the scarcity of women in senior positions in their company. Most were then very cooperative.

They would not have been, however, if I had responded defensively to their sarcasm.

2. ***Ignoring, or the silent treatment.*** Another form of indirect aggression is ignoring others or giving them the silent treatment, by refusing to discuss important issues with them. Some supervisors even refuse to speak to a staff member about anything for days even though they're members of the same department! This is dirty pool and almost as destructive as vindictive sarcasm.

This negative action is a no-win situation for both parties involved. Often the person giving the silent treatment wins the battle, but prolongs the war. If issues are not settled through discussion, they will inevitably resurface later.

Brian felt proud when his department head commended him in front of his co-workers and supervisor for the excellent job he had done on a project. Brian had worked hard to complete the project and felt he deserved the praise. Later that day, he asked his supervisor, Harry, for technical advice relating to his newest project. Harry was very abrupt, and told him to figure it out himself. During the next week, Brian received the "cold shoulder" from Harry, who wasn't as available or supportive as usual. Brian decided to speak to Harry. He said, "I have a problem and I need your help in solving it." He used feedback to explain how he felt when Harry withdrew his help, and asked him to explain why this was happening.

Harry admitted that he was upset when Brian received praise from the department head, and that he felt jealous because this had never happened to him in the past. He promised to be more available in the future.

3. ***Tantrums.***

"How do I deal with my boss? He has tantrums on a regular basis. He slams down the phone, bangs his desk drawers, throws things and slams his office door. I'm completely unnerved by his behavior and became very shaky and nervous. What should I do when this happens in the future?"

People who still resort to temper tantrums as adults haven't completely grown up. A friend advised this employee to picture her boss wearing a bonnet and diaper, sitting in a high chair, banging a spoon on the tray.

She used this stress reliever the next time he had a tantrum and found that bringing forth this humorous mental image kept her from losing her cool with him. She even had the courage one day (after he had settled down) to ask, "Are you finished?"

"Finished what?" he thundered.

"I wondered if you were finished having your temper tantrum?"

He sat quietly for a minute, smiled sheepishly and said, "I guess that's what you would call it, wouldn't you? Yes, I've finished having my temper tantrum."

She did the same thing the next time he had a tantrum, with the same smiling reaction, until finally she didn't have to say anything. He would come to his office door and say, "It's okay now—I'm finished." The beautiful spin-off of this situation was that he soon stopped having tantrums entirely.

Humor can get you through many difficult situations. The above example shows that humor can diffuse anger. Somehow, when we're able to laugh about something, the tension lessens. Use funny mental pictures or even place a favorite cartoon near your desk to remind you to see the funny side of situations.

4. *Sexual harassment.* Sexual harassment is usually thought of as a problem for women in the workplace, but men also have unwanted sexual advances directed at them.

   This work problem has been affecting employees for centuries. Laws pertaining to harassment are changing rapidly. Whether you're a man or a woman, I urge you to investigate your local legislation. Learn about sexual harassment, and how you can reduce it or deal with it. (See Appendix II for where to go for help with sexual harassment.) Research shows that 70 to 80 percent of women have experienced one or more forms of sexual harassment by superiors or co-workers. Fifty-two percent of them lost or left a job because of it.

   The following types of behavior can all be regarded as sexual harassment:

- unwelcome sexual remarks such as jokes, innuendo, teasing and verbal abuse;
- taunts about a person's body, attire, age, marital status;
- displays of pornographic or offensive pictures;
- practical jokes that cause awkwardness or embarrassment;
- unwelcome invitations or requests, whether indirect or explicit;
- intimidation;
- leering or other suggestive gestures;
- condescending or paternalistic treatment that undermines self-respect;
- unnecessary physical contact, such as touching, patting, pinching, punching or physical assault.

A related problem is a type of reverse discrimination that occurs when promotions and bonuses are awarded to an employee in return for sexual favors, while other employees who have earned recognition through good work are passed over.

If you are the object of sexual harassment you should:

1. Tell the person that you object to whatever he or she is doing or saying. Let him or her know you really mean it! If necessary, explain that this behavior could be classified as sexual harassment and you expect it to stop immediately. Keep a written record of occasions when harassment occurs and of what was said when you objected. The record should include dates, times, the names of witnesses, etc.
2. If the harassment occurs again, repeat your earlier objections. Back them up with a written letter or memo. Refer to your earlier spoken complaint. State only the facts. Make *at least three copies* of this letter. Send one copy to the offending person and one to his or her supervisor. Keep one copy for your records. (Additional copies may be sent to your own supervisor and the chief executive officer of your company, if you think it's appropriate.)
3. If the behavior continues, or the company or union fails to deal with it, lodge a formal complaint with your local branch of the Human Rights Commission. When in doubt, call the Human Rights Commission and ask to talk to a trained counselor. If the situation is serious enough, involve the police by lodging a sexual assault charge.

NOTE: If the first incident is serious enough, state your complaint *orally* and in writing (with copies to applicable parties) and lodge a formal complaint with the Human Rights Commission.

Most human rights codes now specify that the person responsible for the act of sexual harassment, plus supervisors, managers, or people in positions of authority who are aware of the sexual harassment and do not take immediate and appropriate action, plus the company in question, may all be named in a complaint brought before the Human Rights Commission.

No longer can others in positions of power look the other way and ignore the fact that sexual harassment is occurring. A supervisor who does nothing about the sexual harassment of an employee is regarded as having condoned the harassment. If the employee knows that the supervisor has observed or is aware of the situation, he or she can include the supervisor in the charge of sexual harassment.

SUPERVISORS WITH DEFICIENT SUPERVISORY SKILLS

Many supervisors, unfortunately, have had little or no supervisory training. Everyone benefits from this kind of training. Even if supervisors have to pay for the training themselves, it's one of the best investments they can make toward their future success.

Supervisors who lack supervisory training can be very frustrating to work for. They may not know how to delegate, how to discipline subordinates, or how to motivate different types of employees. Or, in various ways, they may make it difficult for their staff to operate efficiently. If your supervisor is one of these, you may have to take active steps and suggest the company provide him or her with supervisory training.

1. *Poor delegation*
"My boss is great with people, but is vague at times on how he wants me to do things. He gives unclear directions, then changes his mind the next day."

You'll succeed with this type of boss if you fill in the details of any work he delegates to you. Use paraphrasing to make sure that what he originally says is what you actually hear. If there are any unclear areas, ask questions about what he wants. If he's in the habit of changing his mind the next day, write down the instructions, show the list to him, and confirm his instructions.

Later, show your confusion when he changes his instructions and bring out your list of instructions made earlier. Update the instructions as requested. Soon your supervisor will realize how often he changes his instructions. He may learn to take more time when formulating his requests. This person would probably benefit greatly by attending a time-management course. This would teach him to save time by planning before delegating tasks to subordinates.

Sometimes supervisors are disorganized. They're the ones that explain that they know where everything is on their messy desks. They hate details. This boss hates bad news, so stress what you're going to do about things, rather than dwell on the problem.

"My boss asks me to do things that really aren't my job."

Use paraphrasing to make sure you understand what your supervisor expects from you. Have your job description updated. Then talk with your supervisor to see if someone else can handle a duty that you feel doesn't fit your position.

2. *Obsessive perfectionism*
"My boss is a perfectionist who sometimes expects too much from his staff."

Anticipate your boss's needs. Don't skip details. Give alternatives. Have plans B and C available, should they be necessary. Submit new ideas in writing, including the pros and cons and the alternatives available.

3. *Poor disciplinary technique*
"My boss disciplines me in public."

This is a major *faux pas* on the part of your supervisor. Your first attempt should be to make the person understand and empathize with your feelings. Use the technique of feedback to let the supervisor know how humiliating it is when he or she disciplines you in front of others. Explain that you could accept criticism far more easily if it were given privately. You might have to add that, if you are publicly disciplined in future, you'll simply walk away.

4. *Overorientation toward competition*
"My boss is a very competition-oriented person. He wants me to compete with co-workers and I don't want to."

You may be in the wrong profession. Competing against other employees is the most popular system management uses to encourage staff to make more sales.

Many people respond much better to the challenge of beating their own sales records than to competition with others. Companies should ensure that the standards of competition are fair to those at all levels of experience. If you're new with the company, you can't be expected to compete with someone with an established territory and clientele. Trainees with six months' experience should compete against others in the company with the same experience. Many in sales enjoy competition. Others don't, but are encouraged to set realistic objectives for themselves.

Many sales supervisors can be very stressful to work for. They expect assertive or aggressive behavior from their staff. Pushover behavior is not acceptable. You need to prepare carefully to discuss a problem with such a boss. Be sure you have several workable solutions to suggest before attempting to negotiate changes.

5. *Failure to back up staff*
"My boss doesn't back me up when I get into trouble with clients. She always takes the client's side, and I end up defending myself, even though I'm in the right."

Supervisors who automatically take the client's side in a client–employee dispute are doing their subordinates a grave injustice. Until the employee has had a chance to explain his or her side of the story, the supervisor should remain neutral.

The supervisor should record all the facts given by the client and assure the client that the matter will be investigated.

If your supervisor fails to back you up when you know you're carrying out your duties correctly, use the feedback technique to explain how you feel about being unjustly blamed.

Say, "I have a problem and I need your help in solving it. Last week Mrs. Smith wanted me to bend the rules for her. I explained to her that I had strict guidelines I was expected to follow and said I couldn't do what she wanted. She then spoke to you and got her way. This same thing has happened with four clients in the past month. I felt pretty foolish when she came by my office to tell me she had got what she wanted. I'm wondering if the rules have changed and how I'm to deal with these kinds of problems in the future."

6. *Failure to give credit for special contributions.* I've heard both women and men say (and we'll assume the boss is a man), "I worked all week on that report, and my boss took full credit for it. That's the last time he's going to do that to me!"

When your supervisor "steals" your ideas and takes credit for them, you've made him look good. He needs you to do this. If you don't let him take the credit, he'll hold you back.

For instance, if you write a new policy-and-procedures manual for your department, your supervisor can take full credit for its contents. He has the right (according to the existing rules of business) to use your ideas, and do it with a clear conscience. According to business rules, you (the subordinate) are there to make your supervisor or manager look good. Your ideas become your supervisor's ideas, and the supervisor is not breaking any rules by taking the credit. Most men and women dislike this rule. Many supervisors don't feel that they're doing anything wrong, because "everybody does it."

I disagree completely with this business practice, and encourage supervisors to give credit where credit's due. Supervisors who keep stealing their subordinates' ideas only demotivate them. Chances are, they'll get bad suggestions or no suggestions at all from their staff in the future. If a subordinate has come up with a new method of making a widget, that employee should get the praise and recognition, not the supervisor. What does it matter if the subordinate gets the credit for the good idea? The supervisor could submit the report under his or her name, but give credit to the subordinates who helped prepare the report.

If your supervisor is an old-style limelight-stealer and you can't go along with it, send your new ideas or suggestions to him or her in the form of a memo. Ask for your supervisor's opinion about the merit of your idea. Then it's in writing. Or offer your suggestions at a meeting where others know that it's *your* idea.

"I have to do my boss's work in an acting capacity without extra pay. When he's away, I have to handle his job as well as my own. I don't think this is fair."

Try using the feedback technique to explain your problem. If that doesn't work, look upon the experience as a developmental phase of your employment. Ask your supervisor which duties you can let slide during this double-duty period.

It looks excellent on a résumé when you're able to add "acting supervisory duties while supervisor away." This statement may help you get future supervisory positions. So take the extra work anyway, if you think you can manage to handle two jobs for short periods.

7. ***Interference.*** Dennis had a problem with his manager, Jim. Dennis was new in his position as supervisor of a staff of four. Under the guise of "helping" him, Jim allowed Dennis's staff to bypass Dennis to obtain help directly from him.

Jim was breaking one of the cardinal rules in business by undermining the control and authority Dennis needed to supervise his staff properly. There's a strict rule in business regarding the line of command: managers are not supposed to bypass a supervisor to give work directly to the supervisor's subordinates. Nor should managers get involved in matters of discipline or in performance appraisals that concern the supervisor's staff. Dennis was advised to use the feedback technique to explain that his group's effectiveness was undermined when he had only partial control over his subordinates' work. He should remind Jim that he, Dennis, is ultimately responsible for everything he and his staff do and that he needs full control to do his job effectively.

8. ***Unavailability to staff and clients.*** Shirley asked how she could get her supervisor to tell her where he was. There was an in–out board,

but he seldom used it and often left by the back door. He was seldom available: was either in meetings, out of the office, or sitting behind a closed door.

Shirley was advised to itemize occasions when she had been forced to handle problems on her own and to give her supervisor a list of the difficulties that arose because he wasn't available for consultation. She should then ask her supervisor if there is an alternative supervisor she could consult when he can't be reached.

9. *Failure to respect employees' privacy*
"My supervisor wants to know all about my personal life and I don't want to talk about it."

Say, "I prefer to keep a clear division between my private and business life. I've found it's better for me." If your supervisor pushes further, ask, "Why is my private life so important to you?" The supervisor is thus forced to account for his or her aggressive behavior.

10. *Failure to provide opportunities for growth.* Randy felt frustrated because his supervisor refused to give him assignments that would pre-pare him for his next promotional opportunity. His title was Buyer 1 (the first step on the ladder for the purchasing manager's position). His supervisor, Mel, had been in the Buyer 2 position for five years. He refused to allow Randy to learn anything relating to a future promotion.

In this situation, Mel felt Randy was a "heel-nipper" (someone after his supervisory job), while Randy felt that Mel was "locked into" his position and threatened by Randy's promotional expectations.

Mel didn't understand that his reluctance to prepare Randy for his position was why he wasn't moving ahead in the company. Often, supervisors who have no one ready to take over their position will themselves be overlooked for a promotion. Randy was advised to bring this information to Mel's attention. If that didn't work, he could take a lateral move into a position comparable to his existing one, or try for a promotion in another department.

He was initially reluctant to move to another department because such a move represented a detour from the direct route to the purchas-ing manager's position. When I explained that this might be the only way he could bypass Mel's position, he agreed to try it. He's now the purchasing manager, and supervises Mel.

THE GENTLE ART OF BEING SUPERVISED

An important factor affecting your dealings with your supervisor is your own attitude to supervision. Even the best employees sometimes need guidance and even correction from their supervisor. It is true that there are difficult supervisors who habitually give the necessary guidance in negative form, as criticism. But there are also employees who are too ready to perceive legitimate correction as criticism.

The art of being supervised consists of being able to accept suggestions that will help you improve your performance. Whether these suggestions come to you in the harsh form of criticism or in the milder form of correction or instruction, you need to learn how to handle them in a positive way. The following steps may help you in your effort to learn the delicate art of being supervised.

When your supervisor corrects or criticizes you:

1. Control your thoughts and behavior. Keep in mind that there may be some truth in the criticism (you'll miss it if you concentrate only on how you can defend yourself).
2. Don't respond angrily. Instead, listen carefully to the comments.
3. Ask for specifics if the criticism is vague. For example, if your supervisor says, "I don't like your attitude," ask "What is it about my attitude that concerns you?" Your supervisor might respond with, "Well, you were rude to Mrs. Smith when you served her a few minutes ago. You kept her waiting far too long before you looked after her." You may not like what you hear, but at least now you have something specific to deal with.
4. Use the technique of paraphrasing to confirm your understanding of the problem.
5. If the criticism is valid, apologize and let your supervisor know what steps you'll take to correct the behavior or the problem. Leave guilt

trips behind. Don't let the criticism overwhelm you and affect the rest of your day; instead, simply decide that you won't make the same mistake again.

6. Above all, don't climb into a shell, work to rule or give poor performance should you be criticized for something. We often set up this kind of defense mechanism in ourselves. If we feel that something or someone hurts us (especially a supervisor), we're likely to back off and "lick our wounds."

6

DEALING WITH DIFFICULT CO-WORKERS

In a sense everyone employed by your company is your co-worker, but for the purposes of this chapter "co-worker" refers to employees whose behavior in the workplace affects you, but with whom you have no direct reporting relationship (they do not supervise you; you do not supervise them).

Dealing with difficult co-workers can be tricky, because if you try to get them to change their behavior and don't handle it just right, they may think you're trying to "boss" them. And "bossing" co-workers when you're not their supervisor is, of course, a classic workplace no-no.

As with other groups of difficult people, co-workers' difficult behavior takes a variety of forms.

UNPROFESSIONAL BEHAVIOR

Most employees want to do a good job, and to be important to their companies. People who are committed to doing the best job possible set high standards for their own job performance and earn the right to be very proud of their work. Their consistently professional behavior also brings them the trust and respect of supervisors, clients and co-workers.

The professionalism of your colleagues will, to a large extent, determine whether your workplace is congenial or not. In most work-places, people's jobs are interdependent, and each worker's effective-ness and productivity is usually tied in some way to how well others perform their roles in the company. The unprofessional behavior of one employee can affect the efficiency of many. Although most of us would prefer to live and let live, when a co-worker's inefficiency interferes with our own performance, it is useful to know what sort of action can be taken to correct the problem.

1. Shirkers. Do you have co-workers who don't do their share of the work, but receive more than their share of salary? If you feel this is true, discuss it with your boss. When a "merit system" is implemented fair-ly, companies seldom face this problem.

People may use a variety of tactics to avoid their responsibilities. Being habitually late and being away from their desks are two of the commonest ploys. There are three kinds of time watchers. Let's say all three types have a 10:00 a.m. appointment.

Type 1 people arrive right on the dot of 10:00.

Type 2 people arrive at 10:10 and fully believe they're on time.

Type 3 people arrive at 9:50 and feel they've "just made it!"

Type 2 time-users assume that other people don't mind waiting. This false belief has kept many a person from obtaining a sale, closing a deal and obtaining a contract. People don't like to be kept waiting! They feel that their time is important—and object to being treated as if it isn't.

"I have a friend that I often have lunch with or attend meetings with, but she's always late! Besides using feedback, what else can I do to solve this situation?"

Let her know what the consequences will be should she keep you waiting the next time. Tell her that if she isn't ready when you come for her, you'll leave without her. Then do it! If you are to meet her for lunch, wait only ten minutes before ordering your meal.

George works at a front desk of a government office, and deals directly with the public. Bill, a co-worker, is often late for work. This makes George's job twice as busy, because he has to cover the desk by himself.

Using feedback he said, "Bill, you probably don't realize the double workload I have every time you're late. This makes our department look bad. What do you think you can do to stop this from happening in the future?" (Note that George focused on the consequences for the department, not any personal grievance he felt.)

1. The problem—George has a double workload when Bill is late for work.
2. George's stated feelings or reaction—This makes their department look bad.
3. The solution—George asked Bill to solve the problem.

Betty is a receptionist. One of her duties is to answer the phone for her department. They have in–out boards that all members of the staff are supposed to keep up to date. Unfortunately, one employee, Mildred, leaves her desk, and even the office, without telling Betty where to find her. Nor does she have someone else answer her phone for her when she isn't able to. When clients ask for Mildred, Betty puts the caller through to her desk. If Mildred doesn't answer after the first few rings, the call is returned to her.

Betty said she felt like a fool when she had to explain that she didn't know where Mildred was, or when she would return.

Using feedback, she started the conversation by saying, "I have a problem and I need your help in solving it." Then she asked Mildred what she would suggest to stop the problem from recurring. (This dumps the problem into Mildred's lap, where it belongs.) Mildred still shrugged it off, so Betty added, "I need your cooperation so I can do my job properly for the company. It must appear pretty tacky to the client when I have to admit that I don't know where you are. Can we find some solution that will be acceptable to both of us?"

Betty's persistence eventually produced a compromise that was acceptable to both women. Mildred agreed that she would let Betty know where she was. She arranged for a co-worker to answer her phone when she was away from her desk.

2. Buck-passers. Buck-passers are co-workers who shift their work onto other people's desks. They do this by defining their own responsibilities as narrowly as possible. They are adept at determining why certain tasks are someone else's responsibility.

Shirley reported the following problem: "The gal on the switchboard seems to transfer calls to me when she isn't sure whom the caller should be talking to. I'm too busy with my own work to do part of her work too!"

Shirley should first check her job description to see if that task is part of her assigned duties. If not, she should talk to her boss. She would start the conversation, "I have a problem and I need your help in solving it. Sally, on switchboard, is transferring calls to me when she isn't sure who the caller should be talking to. Am I supposed to do this, or should I suggest she put the calls through to someone else?" This will allow her boss to know what's going on, and to decide what he or she wants Shirley to do about the problem.

Other buck-passers refuse to admit they have made a mistake. They say, "Who me? I didn't do that!" when they know they're at fault.

Deal with this by obtaining as much factual information as you can to prove that the person did do what they did. Again, talk to your supervisor about your concerns over co-workers' failure to take responsibility for their mistakes. Explain that you know anyone can make a mistake, but that it hurts you and other staff if co-workers try to pretend their errors are someone else's fault.

3. Putter-offers. Here are five major types of putter-offers:
1. *Hurry-up Type.* They wait until the last minute and work around the clock to meet deadlines.
2. *I'll Decide Tomorrow.* They postpone decisions until events resolve the situation or a decision is forced on them.
3. *Perfectionists.* They must complete all tasks faultlessly, no matter how insignificant. (These people need to learn to discriminate between important and unimportant assignments.)
4. *I'll Show 'Em.* They delay completing assignments as a way of retaining a sense of personal power and control. This normally happens when they're delegated a task they don't want to do, or feel someone else should do.
5. *Muddler.* They put off work because of bad habits, poor organization or lack of set procedures. They may go in circles, getting less and less accomplished as time goes on. These are the kind of people who start something, but leave it for another task before completing the original one.

Sandy found that at every month end she had to keep after her co-worker Joe to submit information she needed to complete her own report. She'd start reminding Joe a week ahead, then the day ahead. Finally, she went in at the last minute and insisted that he give her the report.

She could try the feedback technique and, if that didn't work, she could submit her report without Joe's information. If it was required information, she should put, "Information not available from ... [Joe's] department." That way, Joe would take the flack, not Sandy.

Another solution would be for Sandy to ask her boss to alleviate the problem. In this case her supervisor would normally talk to Joe's boss to straighten up the difficulty.

AGGRESSIVE BEHAVIOR

The suggestions in earlier chapters on dealing with aggressive behavior will be useful for resolving problems with this type of co-worker. An assertive response is usually the best course of action.

1. Overachievers and competitive types. If some of your co-workers are overachievers who try to make you feel inadequate, do the best you can. Don't let a co-worker try to set standards for you. Performance standards with your company should be based on average performance, not high or overachievers' performance. Speak to your supervisor if you feel the standards of performance are unfair.

Jill had trouble with a co-worker, Sue, who was forever competing with her, even in the most trivial things. For instance, Sue kept challenging Jill to take a typing test with her to see who could type faster. Jill had done this on her noon hour twice already, and found she typed 65 w.p.m. with two errors. Sue typed 80 w.p.m. with eight errors, and felt she was a better typist. In reality, Sue spent much of her time at work correcting her errors. Jill objected when Sue called her a poor sport because she refused to do a third test.

Jill used the feedback technique to let Sue know how she felt about

Sue's competitive approach to things. "Sue, it's not important to me who's the better typist, but I am getting upset because you keep insisting I compete with you. Why do you feel you always have to be the best in everything you do?"

"I like to win."

"Have you ever considered what others might be feeling when you try to force them to compete?"

"Everybody competes."

"Have you checked this out with others?"

"No, I haven't."

"Then maybe you should. I, for one, don't want to compete with others. As long as I'm doing the best job I can, I don't have to know I'm better than others."

Sue didn't concede completely, but thought more about her competitive approach to life. She saved competing for situations that warranted its use. Because she worked in the sales department of her firm, she was able to channel her competitiveness against other companies instead of against her co-workers.

2. Critical types. When others (especially those whom you don't give a hoot about) criticize you unfairly, try the following:

Calmly acknowledge to your critic that there may be some truth in what he or she says. This allows you to receive criticism comfortably, without becoming anxious or defensive, and gives no reward to those using the manipulative criticism. For example:

- *Agree with some aspect of the comment that is true.*
  "You're wearing that awful blouse today."
  "That's right, I am wearing this blouse."
- *Agree that the comment may possibly have some validity.*
  "You're not very careful."
  "Maybe I'm not very careful."
- *Agree with the logic of the comment.*
  "If we bought a new truck now instead of keeping the old clunker, we'd be a lot safer on the road and wouldn't have these high repair bills."
  "You're right. A new truck would have those advantages." (Rather

than, "There you go, another way to spend our money.")
* *Allow for improvement.*
  "Your dresses don't fit you correctly."
  "I'm sure they could fit better."
* *Show empathy.*
  "You're being very unfair."
  "I can see that you feel that I'm unfair."

3. Interrupters. Not all interruptions or interrupters are unjustified. A certain number of interruptions are part of any job, and no one expects co-workers to refrain altogether from social exchanges. It's when interruptions get out of hand that action is needed.

First, keep a log to determine who causes your interruptions, when, and for how long. You may find that a large portion of your day is spent dealing with interruptions. If you feel that they are keeping you from doing your "real" work, you may need to change your attitude. Perhaps dealing with these so-called interruptions is really an important part of your job, as important as completing reports. If that's the case, you need to respond by telling yourself, "That's my job calling."

If, however, your log reveals that many interruptions are not job-related, you need to analyze your findings more closely. Some of these interruptions may be your fault, in the sense that you may appear willing to be interrupted or may be reluctant to tell people you're too busy to talk to them. In this case you need to change your own behavior.

Try doing the following:

* If people just want to chat, suggest they catch you at coffee break.
* Set time limits for meetings, and stick to them.
* Whenever possible meet people in their offices, so you can leave when you want to.

One of Debbie's co-workers used to ignore the fact that Debbie was on the phone and start talking to her. Debbie found it impossible to concentrate properly on her caller because of her co-worker's distracting behavior.

Debbie could have handed her co-worker a piece of paper and a pen, indicating that she could leave a written message. Later, using feedback,

Debbie could explain to her co-worker the difficulties caused by her behavior.

PERSONALITY CONFLICTS

Sometimes the chemistry between you and a co-worker is just wrong. Normally you would just avoid such a person, but personality conflicts can be serious if your jobs require you to work together.

"I don't get along with my co-worker, and my boss won't do anything about the situation. We're at each other's throats all the time."

The first thing you could do is try to get the other employee to talk to you about the problem. You could start by saying, "Jim, we're always at each other's throats. This is affecting our productivity and both our chances for advancement in this company. Can you think of anything we can do to stop the problems we're having?"

If the initial attempt fails, you should then approach your supervisor directly. Start by saying, "I have a problem and I need your help in solving it. Jim and I seem to be on different wavelengths, and we're always at each other's throats. I've tried to resolve our differences, but it doesn't seem to have worked. Can you suggest anything I can do to help us get along better and be more productive?" If the conflict really is affecting your and Jim's productivity, your supervisor needs to be aware of it. It then becomes the supervisor's responsibility to resolve the problem.

CONDUCTING EFFECTIVE MEETINGS

Methods for chairing meetings differ slightly from those for dealing generally with co-workers, because the position of chair gives you some authority over the other participants. However, although the chair has certain powers that other members of the group do not, it is widely agreed that the most successful chairs do not "boss" the meeting. Their job is (a) to make it possible for all participants to contribute their expertise, and (b) to ensure that the purpose of the meeting is accomplished within the allotted time.

If you've ever headed a meeting, you know just how difficult it is to do both these things simultaneously. You want to move things along without missing a valuable contribution. You want to encourage contributions while controlling people who threaten to "take over" the meeting.

There are a variety of techniques that are helpful for dealing with the special problems of meetings. For instance, if someone's too talkative, you can interrupt with, "That's an interesting point. What do the rest of you think about this?" Or "We've been making George do all the work. What do the rest of you think about this?"

If the meeting's in progress and tempers flare, it's the chair's job to emphasize points of agreement and minimize points of disagreement. You can draw attention to the objectives of the meeting or ask direct questions relating to the topic. Or you could invite a contribution from a participant whom you know to be good at resolving disputes: "What do you think, Bill?"

If you suspect, even before a meeting starts, that there will be personality conflicts, talk to those involved before going to the meeting. Ask them to leave their negative attitudes toward each other out of the meeting room.

For instance, let's say you're a team leader for a project where several of your co-workers have to work together in harmony to get the job done. You know that Bill and Jim dislike each other, because they had a heated argument at the last meeting and one of them stormed out. Before the next meeting you might say, "Bill, I've decided to talk to you before the meeting. I'm going to talk to Jim as well. I expect the two of you to participate fully at this meeting and you won't be able to do so if you get upset with each other. Can I count on you to cooperate?"

If you see any reluctance or resistance, you may have to add: "If we have a repeat performance of last week's meeting, I'll have to speak to your manager so we can get this project completed."

Here are some tips to enable you to handle the range of difficult participants you could encounter at a meeting:

Dealing with Problem Participants at Meetings

ACTION	POSSIBLE REASONS	WHAT TO DO
Participant is: Overly talkative—to the extent that other participants do not have an opportunity to contribute	Participant may be: • an "eager beaver"; • exceptionally well informed; • naturally wordy; • nervous.	• Interrupt with "That's an interesting point. . . . Let's see what everyone else thinks." • Directly call on others. • Suggest "Let's put others to work." • When the person stops for a breath, thank him or her, restate pertinent points and move on.
Argumentative—to the extent that others' ideas or opinions are rejected or others are treated unfairly.	• seriously upset about the issue under discussion; • upset by personal or job problems; • intolerant of others; • lacking in empathy; • a negative thinker.	• Keep your temper in check. • Try to find some merit in what's said; get group to see it too, then move on to something else. • Talk to the person privately and point out what his or her actions are doing to the rest of the group. • Try to gain the person's cooperation. • Encourage the person to concentrate on positives, not negatives.
Engaging in side conversations with others in the group.	• talking about something related to the discussion; • discussing a personal matter; • uninterested in the topic under discussion.	• Direct a question to the person. • Restate the last idea or suggestion expressed by the group, and ask for the person's opinion.
Unable to express self so that everyone understands.	• nervous, shy, excited; • not used to participating in discussions.	• Rephrase, restating what the person said, asking for confirmation of accuracy. • Allow person ample time to express self. • Help person along without being condescending.

Always seeking approval.	• looking for advice; • trying to get leader to support his or her point of view; • trying to put leader on the spot.	• Avoid taking sides, especially if the group will be unduly influenced by your point of view.
Bickering with another participant.	• carrying on an old grudge; • feeling very strongly about the issue.	• Emphasize points of agreement, minimize points of disagreement. • Direct participants' attention to the objectives of the meeting. • Mention time limits of the meeting. • Ask participants to shelve the issue for the moment.
Too quiet, unwilling to contribute.	• bored, indifferent, timid, insecure; • more knowledgeable or experienced than rest of the group.	• Direct questions to the person that you're fairly sure he or she can respond to. • Capitalize on the person's knowledge or experience by using him or her as a resource person.
Seeking attention.	• feeling inferior; • hiding a lack of knowledge by clowning around.	• Keep reminding the person about the topic being discussed. • Talk to the person privately. Point out what his or her actions are doing to the rest of the group.
Uninvolved and unwilling to commit to new tasks.	• lazy; • too busy already; • feeling he or she should not have been asked to the meeting in the first place.	• Ask for facts concerning the person's schedule. • Ask the person to volunteer for tasks (others in group must as well). • Make sure you ask the right people to future meetings.

| Already too overcommitted to other things to take on new tasks. | • unaware of own skills and abilities;
• lacking in organizational skills. | • Ask for facts concerning the person's schedule.
• Ask the person whether he or she is already overcommitted.
• Tell the person you're counting on him or her.
• Send the person to a time-management seminar. |
| A buck-passer who blames others for anything negative that happens and doesn't accept new tasks readily. | • unable to admit to making mistakes;
• afraid to take risks. | • Make the person account for his or her actions. Ask for facts to back up allegations.
• Privately ask why the person won't accept new tasks. |

Suppose that you chair a meeting and delegate project assignments to a group. What do you do when you have a follow-up meeting and get these lame excuses?

   a. "I didn't know I was responsible for that!"
   b. "I didn't agree to do that!"
   c. "I thought you didn't need that till next week."

These follow-through techniques may help you ensure that participants follow through too.

1. Set an agenda with time limits (give it to them before the meeting). Then follow the agenda.
2. During the meeting, delegate responsibility as required.
3. Set firm time deadlines for each commitment.
4. At the end of the meeting, ask each individual to confirm that he or she understands the task. "What is it you have to do before our meeting on December tenth? Bill …? Sam …? Sally …?"
5. Follow up with written information (meeting notes).

7

DEALING WITH DIFFICULT SUBORDINATES

UNDERSTANDING THE SUPERVISORY ROLE

There are five essential elements to a supervisor's role. A person with full supervisory status has the responsibility for:

- delegating work
- checking work
- conducting performance appraisals
- disciplining subordinates
- hiring his or her own staff

1. Delegating work. This involves giving tasks to your subordinates for completion.

2. Checking work. This is done to see that employees complete tasks properly. You'll check the quantity and quality of the work performed and how long it took to complete.

3. Conducting performance appraisals. You and nobody else should have the responsibility for doing performance appraisals for all your subordinates. Your manager shouldn't do them, because he or she is not directly responsible for the work of your subordinates. Your manager might review your findings to see if they're fair, but you complete the appraisal on each employee you supervise.

4. Disciplining subordinates. Because your staff ends up making you look either good or bad, you need this control to correct production and/or behavior problems. However, because of the potential dangers of "wrongful dismissal" suits, many companies arrange for the actual firing of employees to be handled by those specially trained in its implementation.

5. Hiring staff. Whenever possible, have as much input as you can into the hiring of people who work for you. If you're on different wavelengths, it can be very difficult for you and your staff to work as a team.

Unfortunately, most employment interviewers decide whether they will hire a person within the first four minutes of the interview. They base their decision on what they see, hear and believe. They're evaluating the person's non-verbal language—how they walk, talk, sit and shake hands—and their verbal communication skills—how well they express themselves, their self-esteem level, etc.

At this point in the interview, the interviewers haven't even begun to ask the questions that should be the determiners of whether they hire the person or not.

If you have the responsibility of hiring staff, keep an open mind until the end of the interview. This way, your decision is based on more concrete information.

How does your supervisory position measure up? If you have only the first two responsibilities, you're in a "lead hand" position. This is a no-win situation for you. If you don't have the responsibility to conduct performance appraisals and discipline staff, you'll receive only token respect from your subordinates and will have little control over the outcome of their work.

If you don't have that control over your employees, and they do an unsatisfactory job—who looks bad? You do! If your company puts you in this position, talk to your manager and ask that you have the first four responsibilities (and the fifth, if at all possible). If your request is refused, ask that the manager look after the delegation and checking of responsibilities as well, and explain your reasons.

SUPERVISING FORMER PEERS

How should you handle the first day on the job where you're suddenly responsible for supervising your former peers? You'll likely fail if you don't handle that first day or week properly. It's necessary to remove any feelings of envy and jealousy your new subordinates might have.

Your manager will usually call a meeting to introduce you to your new staff, then leave so you can take over the meeting.

If you anticipate hard feelings, deal with your former co-workers' feelings first. Start by saying, "I know a few of you applied for and wanted this promotion. I can understand that you may feel a little upset that I got the position instead of you. The company chose me, so what we do from now on depends on how all of us work together. I need your support to handle my job properly. In return, I'll do everything I can to be a good supervisor. Can I count on you for your support?"

Ask those present, one by one, to indicate to you whether you can rely on them: "Margie—how about you, can I count on your support?" "Dave?" Cover every employee in the room. If your staff have made an oral commitment to you, they're much more likely to cooperate in the future.

If you detect reluctance to make the commitment, don't let it pass. In a private interview, say, "Margie, I detect some hesitancy in your reply. What can I do to make the situation a little easier for you?"

If she still balks, you'll have to keep your eye on her. She might try to sabotage your efforts. If she does, you'll have to be on top of the situation and implement immediate disciplinary action. Don't be afraid to do it. Nip the problem in the bud; don't let it grow and flourish and contaminate the others in your section.

DELEGATING

Many supervisors fail because they lack the ability to delegate tasks properly to their staff. They make excuses such as:

- "I need this completed right now. I could finish this job and three others if I did it myself. It would take twice as long to train someone else, then check to see they did it right!"
- "This job is so important that only I can do it."
- "I'm afraid my staff will fail."
- "I can do this better than anyone else."
- "I don't want my people to think I'm a tyrant."

Many hidden reasons are behind the above explanations. Supervisors don't delegate enough tasks because:

- They fear a loss of control. It reflects directly on them if their staff goofs up.
- They fear losing their jobs. Some supervisors feel that if they delegate too much, they'll have no job left to do. Another expression is, "Suppose someone on my staff becomes better than me?"

Many supervisors are unaware of an important factor in delegation. Failure to groom staff to succeed them may result in their being overlooked themselves when a more responsible position is being filled. Proving there is someone ready to take over their existing position is one way of showing they are eligible for promotion. (One way to prove this is to ensure there is at least one employee who can be placed in an acting position when the supervisor is away.)

MOTIVATING EMPLOYEES

Of course, much more is involved in supervision than simply assigning and checking work, assessing performance and disciplining employees. Supervising people is an art that depends to a great extent on how well you can motivate people.

Supervisors must watch for the "Pygmalion effect" when trying to motivate staff. If a supervisor believes employees are smart, he or she will treat them that way. If a supervisor believes employees are capable of independent thought, he or she will treat them that way. Unfortunately if the supervisor believes that they are lazy, dumb or slow to pick up new ideas (or have any other undesirable attribute), he or she often treats them that way too. People respond to what they perceive is wanted from them. If supervisors expect high achievement, that's likely what they'll get. If supervisors expect low productivity, that's likely what they'll get.

Do you need to change your attitude toward the abilities of your staff? Are you letting the Pygmalion effect influence how you supervise your staff?

Some people are motivated by their interest in the work itself. Other motivators are the desire or need for:

- money
- acceptance by peers
- competition/challenge
- awards
- status
- better working conditions
- job security
- promotional opportunities
- a better office
- extra benefits
- recognition for good work

It's possible that your employees hear from you only when they've made mistakes. It's normal for all of us to want to receive praise and recognition for work well done. It's the best motivator of all. Give it a try. See if things change.

Be aware that it's not possible to motivate everyone—you just *can't* motivate some people. With unsatisfactory workers, start by spelling out exactly what you expect of them (document your requests properly). Then give them ample opportunity to improve their performance. If they refuse to conform, replace them with good workers. There are too many excellent people who are unemployed for companies to keep foot-draggers on the payroll. They just demotivate everyone around them.

Acquaint yourself with some of the standard procedures for managing human resources and try to get your company to use them, if it is not already doing so. Such basic tools of personnel management as job descriptions and performance appraisals help employees feel that they know what is expected of them and that their efforts are recognized. They can be confident that procedures are in place to allow them to develop their skills and earn promotions. The advantages of some of these management tools are discussed in the examples that follow.

1. Standard motivational management tools.
"My staff expect to receive credit for their contribution to my reports and projects."

As mentioned in the chapter on dealing with supervisors, the boss's failure to give them credit is a pet peeve of subordinates. It certainly can't hurt you if you give your staff credit for doing part of a report or project, can it? If you don't, you'll probably have demotivated them for the next report or project they're part of. The main goal of supervisors is to motivate staff to do their best work. Doesn't it make sense to give them credit for good work?

"My staff expects me to change their job descriptions to suit their own talents and abilities!"

Many progressive-thinking firms are doing just that. Instead of pushing employees to fit the needs of the company, many are adapting positions to match the employees' talents and abilities. Until all firms do this, employees must conform to the needs of the position they're hired to fill.

"I don't fully believe in job descriptions because they just encourage staff to state, 'That's not in my job description!'"

As discussed earlier, accurate, up-to-date job descriptions are essential for an employee to do good work. How can your staff possibly do a good job for you and your company if they don't know what's expected from them? Clearly define each task, giving standards of performance (quality, quantity and time) for each one. Then, and only then, will both you and your staff know what's expected of them.

"My training budget is nil, but my staff want and expect training."

It's not a nice place for a supervisor to be, but it happens in bad economic times. It's not always possible for companies to provide all the funds for training, but there can usually be some compromises. Some companies have employees sign a document stating that employees will have to reimburse their company for the cost of training, should they leave the company within two years of training. Alternatively, the company could pay for half the training costs.

If employees require training, the supervisor must show management the cost-effectiveness of the training. Itemize the ways in which the training will benefit the company. In particular, try to identify the financial benefits to the company. If the company still proves ungenerous, encourage staff to get the training themselves. Explain the benefits to them of additional future salary as compared to the cost of training— that it's an investment in their future.

"My staff want regular performance appraisals, but my company doesn't give them."

It's a standard practice in most businesses to have at least a yearly performance appraisal for each employee. As well, appraisals are often conducted at the end of the employee's probationary period. They're highly recommended, to make employees aware of how they're doing. Some firms offer performance appraisals after each special project.

There are many kinds of performance appraisals. Most are extremely poor because they evaluate subjective things such as attitude, judgment and initiative. This type of evaluation depends heavily on the mood of the person preparing the appraisal.

Instead, employees should be evaluated on whether they reached planned objectives. Each objective would include standards of performance. This method takes the uncertainty out of performance appraisals. Both the employee and the supervisor know exactly how the employee is doing because the evaluation is based on facts rather than on the supervisor's personal impressions.

If your company doesn't have regular performance appraisals, suggest it start to do so. State that you intend to have such appraisals for your own staff, even if the company doesn't. In many cases, when one department initiated an appraisal system, employees in other departments soon saw the benefits and lobbied for the system to be used company-wide. Try it—you've got nothing to lose.

"My company doesn't have a personnel department. How do I choose proper salary ranges for my staff?"

Call your competitors and find out what they pay people with skills and abilities like those of your staff. Watch newspaper advertisements describing positions like those in your company. Don't be cheap—it's better to overpay slightly than to underpay and lose good employees.

"Should I follow the trend of replacing older, more expensive staff with younger, less expensive staff?"

This is a tough question to answer. It's often the only answer some companies see to economic problems. A senior, long-term employee who may be five years away from retirement and earns $40,000 could be replaced by a more junior person at $30,000 a year.

Many companies have been offering their senior staff early retirement, as a humane compromise. Some firms, however, simply decide to let their senior, more expensive staff go. Not only is this usually devastating for the employee, but other staff soon begin to wonder when their turn will come. Employees the company may wish to keep may seek other jobs and leave at inconvenient times. Morale may suffer and affect productivity adversely.

Though there aren't any easy answers to this problem, companies need to consider the pros and cons very carefully before deciding to follow this trend.

2. Motivating aggressive employees.
A real test of a supervisor's skill are employees who appear to be poor-

ly motivated but have the potential to be great assets to the company. Such employees often have a great deal of energy that shows itself in negative, aggressive, even trouble-making behavior. This negative behavior could be caused by:

- the feeling that they lack job security;
- the feeling that they lack the necessary education, experience or knowledge;
- lack of self-esteem or pride in their own skills, abilities and achievements;
- work that underuses their skills and abilities;
- the feeling of not fitting in with their work group (perhaps because of racial and/or cultural differences).

Those who believe they don't fit into their positions for whatever reason may act aggressively toward their company, top management, supervisors, co-workers or clients. Supervisors seeking to "turn around" employees of this type could:

- give authentic compliments on the work completed;
- explain to the employees how valuable their efforts are to their fellow workers (part of the team);
- explain the importance of their jobs to the company;
- show that their training and other qualifications equip them to do more than just a satisfactory job;
- provide some measure of recognition for their work accomplishments;
- bring them into group situations: ask for their advice;
- carefully describe the responsibilities of their position and set *reachable* performance standards.

Many aggressive employees have a great deal to offer. They may be very success-oriented and willing to accept challenges and to set high standards for themselves in order to achieve recognition. Their energy level is often high, so that supervisors may find it difficult to keep them constructively occupied. Power also stimulates these people, and they may respond well if given some authority as soon as they're able to handle it. Delegate responsibilities that allow them to take charge, but watch carefully for abuse of other co-workers or clients. These employees may be poor delegators and unwilling to ask for the help that they need. They may prefer to work alone. Give them that chance if possible. Such employees also tend to enjoy variety, so try to change their tasks often.

3. Motivating employees who are reluctant to change.

When supervisors want to make changes in the methods their subordinates use to complete assignments, they're often surprised by the resistance they meet. This is especially true right now with so many technological changes happening.

Do you have trouble adjusting to change? Can you think of a situation that's facing you now that involves change? If you're able to identify one, ask yourself, "What can go wrong if I refuse to change?" Then decide what the advantages will be of changing now, rather than later, when you have no choice.

Supervisors and trainers need to be aware of the stages people go through when adjusting to change in order to help them make the transition as smoothly as possible. There are three phases in the process:

1. *Unfreezing.* During this initial stage you require employees to give up their regular way of doing things and identify new methods. This involves breaking old habits.
2. *Changing.* The new pattern of behavior or new way of doing something is explained and taught. Before this can be done the supervisor needs to identify the advantages of the change and the reasons why it might provoke resistance. Ways of overcoming objections to the change should also be identified.
3. *Refreezing.* Employees use of the new method is monitored until it takes hold. Supervisors must catch die-hards who are determined to do it the old way. This can take up to three months of constant surveillance.

Overcoming Objections to Change

New systems, methods and designs won't work unless you get people to accept new ideas. You might have to sell your ideas. This is where planning comes in. For example, suppose you've found a faster way of processing clients' orders. Before explaining the new system to others, prepare by:

a. writing a summary of the existing method;
b. determining the advantages and disadvantages of this method;
c. writing a summary of the new method;
d. determining the advantages and disadvantages of the new method;
e. anticipating the objections others will raise and deciding what you will say to defend your new idea.

The following checklist will help you cope with objections from others more effectively.

- Anticipate and prepare for as many possible objections as you can. Develop a plan for handling each of them.
- Ask staff to explain their objections in very specific terms with examples.
- Don't be content with superficial reasons for resistance to a change. Dig until you discover the real reasons.
- Work out a practical way of overcoming each objection if you possibly can.
- If you're unable to overcome an objection, try to find a way to compensate for it.
- Rally enough benefits to win the person's support and cooperation despite the objection.
- Find a way to ease the person's mind, to make it less risky to go along with you despite the objection.
- With habitual or chronic objectors, introduce your idea gradually. Don't try to get immediate acceptance or compliance. The objection may be nothing more than a delaying tactic—the person's natural resistance to change.
- Consider bringing up significant objections yourself instead of waiting for others to do so. Then explain how these can be overcome.

CORRECTING OR DISCIPLINING EMPLOYEES

Sometimes supervisors have to correct their employees' behavior. Whether the outcome is positive or negative depends on how they do this. There are two basic kinds of criticism: constructive and destructive.

1. *Constructive Criticism.* Constructive criticism attempts to correct the behavior of the person. The person offering the criticism explains how he or she feels about the behavior that needs to be changed and gives the other person a chance to correct the behavior. For example, "Joan, I'm finding that your gum-cracking is distracting me from doing my work. Would you like this roll of peppermints instead?"

2. *Destructive Criticism.* Destructive criticism focuses on the person rather than the behavior. For example, "Joan, stop cracking your gum! You're the most selfish person I know! You don't care anything about the people who have to work with you!"

   Joan probably feels the need to defend herself (she has been personally attacked). She'll probably retaliate, and her negative behavior will likely continue.

The following communication skills are useful when it's necessary to discipline or criticize a subordinate.

Supportive questions

These are responses that show acceptance and understanding of the feelings of the person you're talking with, and acknowledge his or her efforts to grow and change.

1. "Do you feel you're not getting co-operation from …?"
2. "How can I help you get this roadblock removed?"
3. "You believe you have the skills to complete this task?"

Exploratory questions

These are responses made to encourage further examination even though the facts may be unpleasant.

1. "Tell me more about that."
2. "What seems to be the difficulty here?"
3. "When did this first start?"
4. "How does this relate to your performance?"

"I never know how to start an interview where I have to correct someone's behavior. Should I start by telling the person all their good qualities and attributes, before I concentrate on the ones I want changed?"

Start by giving a brief overall summary of the employee's behavior (trying to emphasize the good-news aspect), then discuss the behavior you want to correct, and end by refocusing on the employee's strengths.

Think back to conversations you've had with former bosses. Did you hear one word they said while they were expressing their views on what you did right? Probably not. We seem to wait for that special word "but," and we seldom hear anything that precedes it. Most people do things right about 95 percent of the time, but feel hurt about the 5 percent that requires correction.

Because of this, you should start by talking about the 5 percent they have done wrong. Explain that the important thing is that they learn from their mistakes and don't make them again. Then you can use the rest of the interview to tell them what they've done right. This concludes the meeting with positive feelings and results in a more pleasant ending for both of you. The employee knows what has to be corrected, but isn't left with a feeling of failure.

DEALING WITH UNPRODUCTIVE BEHAVIOR

The term "unproductive behavior" covers a multitude of items, from intractable inefficiency to theft. To correct some of these you need little more than well-honed communication skills. Others may require you to exercise all the supervisory and managerial skills at your command.

1. Buck-passing employees.

In today's complex managerial environment, it's becoming increasingly important to avoid even minor errors. Buck-passing can be a symptom of a supervisor's failure to delegate responsibility correctly or to define responsibilities clearly. Formal policy-and-procedures manuals that define responsibility would eliminate some of this buck-passing.

It's not enough for supervisors to tell employees how to do their jobs. They must also explain exactly what their responsibilities are. For example, "Wilma, you're responsible for correctly matching freight bills to the duplicate of the receiving report."

"What if there are differences?"

"It's part of your duty to note the differences on the voucher to Accounts Payable. Any mistakes in matching will be your fault. Any questions?"

Even a well-qualified employee like Wilma will make mistakes. However, she'll make fewer and fewer mistakes and won't attempt to pass the buck if you keep reminding her of her responsibilities.

Try not to overdiscipline for any errors. Too heavy a disciplinary hand only invites excuses (e.g., "The dispatcher said it's okay to approve trucking bills, so I thought this was okay too." Or: "Don't blame me for that one! John said it was okay to approve it.").

Overly severe disciplinary action for mistakes has other adverse effects besides buck-passing. It causes lying, cheating and hiding of mistakes. The concealment of mistakes causes irreparable harm to the company. Service failures can be expensive. The cost of the immediate replacement of the service plus the lowered image of the company results in decreases in sales or service volume.

From time to time, supervisors should set an example by admitting to mistakes themselves in the presence of their subordinates. This can demonstrate to others that passing the buck is not acceptable.

2. Bottleneck employees.

"The work isn't getting out because John's sitting on it!" Bottlenecks are a frequent management complaint. A bottleneck is someone or something that stops the flow of work. It often results in employees' inactivity while they wait for the bottleneck to clear. The causes could be attributable to either the design of the work flow or the employee's personal work habits. If you suspect poor design of the work flow, try this simple test. Have another employee assume the duties of the employee in the problem area. If there's still a bottleneck (after a period of training), make changes in the work-flow arrangement.

Bottleneck employees typically have the following characteristics:

- tendency to be derailed by relatively minor problems;
- not enough training;
- low decision-making capability;
- ignorance of productivity requirements;
- lack of team-member identity;
- job insecurity;
- unusual fear of making mistakes;
- incompatibility with co-workers leading to lack of cooperation.

If there's no indication that the bottleneck is deliberately caused, perhaps the bottleneck employee is not clear about what you want. The supervisor should reinforce the employee's training. During this retraining, the supervisor can see if the employee is comprehending the job in detail, demonstrate to the employee how to perform the various tasks and then guide the employee under direct observation. The emphasis should be on techniques that can speed up completion of the job.

Employees should know how their job fits in with others in the company. They then have knowledge of the consequences of their own good or bad performance.

Most stick-in-the-mud employees don't really want to be that way. Most want to feel that they are cooperating in achieving common goals. The secret is to make everyone in the workforce have a common goal. Supervisors should enlist the help of other employees by saying:

"Say, Tom, can you show Richard how we can move that project faster?"

"Richard, let Tom show you a couple of techniques for pushing the stuff through that we need now."

An important element in removing the bottleneck is to make the employee want to put the work out faster. The paying of a few compliments here and there improves confidence among slower employees. It permits them to have a greater feeling of job security and certainly reduces tensions. The bottleneck employee who feels more in control will have less fear of making mistakes. In short, some additional coaching, coupled with a reduction in tension, may free the employee to move faster.

3. Error-prone employees.

There are two basic kinds of accidents. One type results from systems design. The methods or techniques used permit a certain number of errors. Constant improvement of the system reduces the error rate. However, no matter how well the system is designed, the human factor must be considered as well. The following conditions may be at fault:

- inadequate job training;
- limited written instructions;
- too many subordinates reporting to one supervisor;
- too few intermediate levels of supervision;
- dull work environment;
- employees bored with their jobs;
- no studies done to determine error causes;
- high employee-turnover rate.

Auto-insurance companies recognize that some drivers are more prone to having accidents than the general population of drivers. Some employees are more likely to make mistakes than others. Deliberate mistakes should result in disciplinary actions, up to and including firing of the employee. However, most mistakes aren't intentional. They're caused by a variety of factors, including errors in judgment on the part of management or lack of employee training. Suggested steps to reduce errors are:

1. Determine the nature of errors.
2. Revise the system to improve error detection.
3. Use a senior employee as a coach to an error-prone employee.
4. Appeal to the employee's pride of workmanship.

5. Have a chat with an error-prone employee to review causes of mistakes.

Most employees like to feel that they're earning their pay. Part of that feeling of pride stems from their opinion that their work has few, if any, errors. Therefore, they appreciate help, when it is offered gracefully, in improving their own pride in their work. One method of attack is to provide an employee-coach for the error-prone employee.

Senior employees who are proficient in their work can help isolate the *causes* of problem employees' errors. Rather than catching mistakes *after* the fact and taking corrective action, they can provide instruction to help avoid errors. The problem employee may simply need to be told which points require additional attention (e.g., "Bryan, can you spend a little more effort on rechecking?" or, "Marcia, can you pay a little more attention to these types of items?").

To reinforce pride of workmanship, don't let employees describe their positions as "just a janitor" or "just a receptionist." Be ready to explain their importance to the smooth running of your company.

4. Daydreamers.

We all daydream, but some people do it to excess—to a point where it results in low productivity, errors and accidents. Some jobs lend themselves more to employee daydreaming than others and need more thorough monitoring.

It's not always fair to pin the blame for daydreaming on employees. Their jobs may be so boring that they can't keep their minds on the task. Robotic-like duties invite employee daydreaming.

Work that requires employee creativity should have an environment that's conducive to creativity. Where different and varied types of work proceed through a section, it's advisable to use job rotation to alleviate monotony. Adding flexibility in the method of performing the job will allow the employees to decide how to handle individual steps. Such flexibility permits employees to think about how they want to handle particular jobs. This in turn increases alertness and reduces monotony. The use of job rotation provides some cross-training (more people know different jobs). This gives supervisors a greater flexibility in the use of their staff and provides more than one worker who is qualified to fill the position.

Jobs should be designed to hold the employee's attention. Tasks performed while the person is standing discourage daydreaming. Better design of the work area can also help. The decor of the work area is of some importance. Desks or work areas need not be the same color. Make every effort to remove monotony in the work environment. Recommended steps are:

1. Evaluate the environment. Make any changes possible.
2. Revise work flow to reduce monotony.
3. Develop alternative methods and order of steps to accomplish the work.
4. Where possible, let the employee decide what he or she is to produce that day.
5. Identify employees who require constant supervisor prompting to improve attentiveness.

No matter what efforts you make to dispel daydreaming, some employees remain lost in the clouds. Only constant supervisory attention can dispel the problem and keep the employee on his or her toes. In this case, a discussion between the supervisor and the employee is definitely in order. It may become necessary to replace the worker.

5. Time-wasters.

a. Personal telephone calls

Nothing's as annoying to a supervisor as watching an employee receive an excessive number of personal telephone calls. It's not just that the lines are being tied up; the flow of work is also interrupted. If employees waste company time, they waste the company money allotted for their salaries. Employees should keep personal calls to a minimum. After all, they are at a place of business, and personal-life requirements should wait until after work.

Employees who conduct personal business on company time are often overlooked for promotions. Most don't even understand what they've done to hamper their progress in the company.

Strategies to alleviate this problem include:

1. Telling employees to limit personal phone calls to important or emergency calls, which should be kept short and sweet. Have them

advise their friends and relatives about the company policy. No more than one or two personal calls a day should be necessary.

2. Requiring the switchboard operator to ask an incoming caller for his or her name and to say, "What company do you represent?" That question alone may be enough to reduce non-business calls and their duration. The switchboard operator might keep track of non-business calls for one or two days and submit a report to the supervisor of each section. Interviews with errant employees can then be arranged to reinforce the policy.

3. Making sure employees realize that their behavior may be keeping them from being promoted to a higher position.

b. Coffee- and lunch-break abuses

Studies show that breaks in the work schedule increase production. At the same time, supervisors need to guard against the tendency of employees to slow down in anticipation of coffee or lunch breaks. Many employees will extend their breaks if there is no pressure on them not to do so. After the break, work should begin right away. If you've identified this as a problem, be visible immediately before and after breaks. This enables you to observe abuses directly and to encourage more productive use of your employees' time. After the break, you could hand out assignments or check employees' progress.

Only a conscientious effort on the part of supervisory personnel will segregate those who occasionally abuse breaks from those who consistently do so. Despite supervisory efforts, some employees will continue to abuse coffee and lunch breaks. This warrants formal disciplinary action (written warning in file, suspension for a day, etc.).

c. Absenteeism

Many employees will go to work even with a runny nose and a fever. They refuse to take advantage of their company's sick-pay policy. Many feel they don't wish to take sick leave for minor ailments because they may need the leave when they're really sick. Others feel that no one else can handle their job as well as they can. They feel responsible for their performance. To them, it's part of the ethic of being a good worker. The supervisor should recognize the sacrifices made by this kind of worker.

When that type of employee is out ill, he or she is usually too sick to perform any kind of work at all. Such employees are assets to any company. Unfortunately, however, most companies also have their share of employees who abuse their sick-leave privileges. In fact, *in any normal working day, usually from 4 to 6 percent of all employees are absent from work.*

Absenteeism disrupts the flow of work and causes delays and production problems. The quality of work suffers because employees replaced by others are not as well trained or because overtime is needed to complete the extra work.

Because the costs to the company of abuses of sick leave are high, all supervisors need to take steps to discourage unwarranted absenteeism. Such steps include:

- enforcing the rules. Otherwise employees will keep on abusing them, and others may be encouraged to do so as well;
- determining if there are absenteeism patterns. The five major types of unwarranted absenteeism are listed below along with some strategies for dealing with them. (NOTE: Some solutions may not be compatible with your company's union agreements. Make sure you're aware of these before acting.)

(i) Chronic absenteeism

Chronic absentees are often negative thinkers. Everyday frustrations and pressures easily overwhelm them. They consistently have unwarranted absences that usually follow a pattern. This type of employee calls and says, "Sorry, boss, but I can't make it in today." You may be tempted to reply, "I'm sorry you're sick. Stay away until you're feeling better." However, don't say that. Don't worry, such employees will stay away until they feel a lot better, with or without your blessing. They view their sick leave as a right.

How many times a year do employees pull that line before you consider them chronic absentees? One company identifies problem employees by eight or more absences of one or more days each month in a year.

For those suspected of abusing their sick-leave privileges, the supervisor should call the employee at the end of each work day and say, "Orson, how are you coming along? I'm calling to see if you expect to be back to work tomorrow."

Using this tactic allows two beautiful spin-off benefits to happen. First, you've determined that the absent employee is really at home. Of course, he or she could have been at the doctor's, but not *every* time you called. Second, you will discourage the employee from taking sick leave for minor ailments or to accomplish personal chores.

When the employee returns to work, the supervisor should:

- state, "Sure missed you yesterday. We really need and depend on you."
- describe the problems the employee's absence caused the department.
- encourage the employee to be in more often.
- explain the consequences if similar instances occur too often.

Innocent absenteeism, even if it's excessive, doesn't warrant disciplinary action. On the other hand, an employee's inability to report regularly for work, *for whatever reasons*, provides grounds for termination of employment. In such cases:

1. The employer must be able to document the employee's absences. These absences must be well beyond what any reasonable person would consider acceptable. The employee must have deviated substantially and unduly from the average level of attendance of other employees.
2. The employer must be able to demonstrate that the excessive-absenteeism problem has been persistent. It must have continued despite *documented* attempts by the employer to have it corrected. The supervisor must keep a record of his or her efforts to counsel the employee and to determine the underlying reasons for absences. The supervisor must be able to show that he or she has been compassionate and has taken extenuating circumstances into account.
3. The employer must be able to present convincing reasons explaining why he or she feels there's little or no likelihood of improvement.

An employee who falsifies a doctor's certificate should receive a written warning, which is placed on his or her file, or possibly termination. The degree of discipline depends on the circumstances.

If an employee is absent for more than three days in a row without calling in, it can be assumed that he or she has abandoned the job. This could result in dismissal.

When an employee's excessive absenteeism is due to a drinking problem, the employer may discharge the employee. The employer must be able to demonstrate that the employment relationship cannot continue. The company must be able to defend its decision and show that it has recognized the alcoholic problem as an illness. It must be able to prove that it has made an honest effort to help the employee to correct the illness.

(ii) Goof-off absenteeism

These absentees typically decide to enjoy themselves (go golfing, perhaps) rather than do what they consider dull, repetitive work that they believe wastes their abilities. They feel the need to escape the humdrum environment of work. This can lock them into a vicious circle, because these people are seldom considered for the promotions they think they need and deserve. To help them lose this need to escape, the supervisor should:

1. Confront them with their absenteeism record.
2. Ask why it's happening.
3. Encourage them to use their sick leave properly. Explain that SICK LEAVE IS A PRIVILEGE, NOT A RIGHT and should be used for *their own* authentic illnesses, *not for personal reasons or their children's or spouse's illnesses.*
4. Make sure that they are aware that their absence record is a major factor keeping them from being promoted.
5. Identify rewards (e.g., a promotion) that may be obtained with good attendance. This is far better than using punishment (written warning on file) to bring about changes in behavior.

(iii) Naive absenteeism

Many employees believe that management expects and condones phoney absences. These employees also believe that if they have sick leave coming, they have the right to take it whenever they please. Employee morale breaks down when employees get away with calling in sick and get paid for the day, when they weren't sick at all. While it's difficult to determine with complete certainty who is truly ill and who isn't, supervisors should make sure that employees don't abuse sick leave. To deal with this, supervisors should:

1. Confront employees regarding their absenteeism record.
2. Explain what sick leave is all about (a privilege, not a right). Tell them that they're doing important work and that the company suffers when they're away.
3. Encourage employees to use absences properly—for legitimate illnesses.
4. Ask employees to identify what effects their absence has had on other employees.

(iv) Abusive absenteeism

Some employees will be away for any and every minor ailment. They demonstrate little sense of responsibility for any required productivity. It is of little concern to them if their absence means that other workers have to carry a larger workload or that their company will suffer economically. These employees are usually unhappy, feel victimized and believe that others receive favoritism. They break company rules and have many conflicts with their supervisors. They pick fights and believe that they're always right and others are always wrong. Should you have to deal with such employees:

1. Be direct about the penalties for continuing the abuse. "Your job's on the line unless you conform to the rules of this company." Tell them you'll have to replace them if their record doesn't improve, that they must produce doctor's reports for absenteeism, etc. Stick to the facts and be firm and clear about the consequences.
2. Compliment them on the work they do when they are conforming to the rules.

(v) Legitimate absenteeism

Authentic illnesses, bereavement, jury duty and necessary personal business, such as dentist and doctor's appointments, are legitimate reasons for taking time off. However, employers shouldn't pay sick leave to those who take time off for their children's illnesses (this should be time off without pay, unless company policy states otherwise).

Absenteeism Policies

When industries rely on individual performance, any absence is a disruption in the flow of service to customers. To help reduce absenteeism, many companies have implemented stiffer proof-of-illness procedures. They may:

- require a doctor's certificate for any absence of three or more sick days a week;
- require a doctor's certificate for *any* absence due to illness, or after a holiday weekend;
- require a complete physical examination by the company doctor if the employee is away more than ten days in any one year.

6. Poor housekeepers.

Many consider good housekeeping as window dressing. They explain, "I know where everything is on my desk!" It's when they're away because of illness that their messiness causes difficulties. Others who take over can't find things. In fact, poor housekeepers often *don't* know where everything is, and an unduly messy work area may be a sign of inefficiency. Excessive untidiness can result in:

- missing records or files;
- lost or misplaced tools or equipment;
- high supply costs;
- an improper mix of parts and inventory;
- contamination of the product;
- high scrap and reworking costs;
- a poor balance of finished products in inventory;
- high machine downtime;
- a poor safety record;
- low employee morale and reluctance to work overtime;
- discipline problems and labor turnover.

Motivate your employees to maintain a tidy work area by your example. Good housekeeping habits are more easily encouraged among your staff if your own office is kept neat and clean. Encourage clean-ups at the end of each day. If you spot employees whose work stations look messy heading for the door, stop them. Ask them to organize their work station before leaving. You may have to provide a written checklist of housekeeping activities they are to follow.

7. Dishonest employees.

There was a time when thefts from inventory affected only industries that had attractive types of inventory. Increasingly, however, all types of inventory are becoming subject to theft. Not only completed assemblies, but also parts and even raw materials are being stolen.

Employees who take home a few colored pencils for their children may not cost the company much but they set a bad attitudinal example. Some employees go far beyond a few pencils. Theft is often a way of "getting back at management." Some of these people will steal far more than they could ever use. Usually, employees who constantly steal are unsatisfactory employees, not only because of their thieving, but for other reasons as well. It's not just that they have low regard for company property, but they think little of the company that employs them.

It's not economically justifiable to lock everything up, nor is it possible to catch all the culprits. However, if management removes some of the temptations, they'll have fewer losses. Having only or two people in charge of the company office supplies is one way of cutting down on pilfering. Having employees sign for stationery and equipment is another.

DEALING WITH PERSONALITY CLASHES

When two of your staff have a personality clash, how and when should you intervene?

If two employees don't get along, the one who suffers most is their supervisor. You may find that Bob and George are excellent workers, but harass each other and fail to cooperate. If the conflict arises from a work-related cause and affects their productivity or that of others, the supervisor will have to help the employees resolve their disagreement. Frequently though, the cause is something related to the basic nature of the two personalities involved. Even the cleverest supervisors can't change people's personalities. The most they can hope to do is to get the two employees to work reasonably well together despite their admitted personality differences.

One recommended method is to call both parties into a private office. Let both in turn state what they think the problems are and blow off a little steam. Then act as an impartial mediator whose only interest is to keep up production. *You must let these employees know that you will not tolerate the situation as it is.*

Encourage the employees to discuss ways of resolving the problem and to agree on a course of corrective action. Keep a close watch on the situation and call further interviews if warranted. Make sure both employees know what the consequences will be if their negative behavior continues.

DEALING WITH EMOTIONAL PEOPLE

If we've caused a person to feel badly and he or she reacts emotionally, we normally comfort that person—and rightly so. In the workplace, however, you need to keep your distance from staff who become emotional. For example, you may be a supervisor who has the unpleasant task of disciplining, dismissing or laying off an employee. Perhaps the person is in tears and very embarrassed about it. How can you make this situation easier for both people?

One of my tasks when I worked in human resources was the chore of laying off or firing employees. Because I'm a real softy, I would occasionally become emotional along with the person being laid off disciplined. By accident, I found a way of helping both of us regain our equilibrium.

I achieved this when I handed the person a box of tissues and said, "I have something I have to attend to. I'll be back in a few minutes."

Then I left the room and took a few deep breaths. When I felt I had my emotions under control, I went back to my office.

Because I had given the person the same opportunity to calm down, she had regained her composure and some of her self-respect. We were able to continue the conversation until we took care of all the issues.

Save using this tactic for situations that warrant it. Many people use tears to get sympathy and will try to manipulate you with their tears. When dealing with this type, I give them a box of tissues and continue the conversation.

DEALING WITH RACIAL AND ETHNIC SLURS

Most workforces, if they're in compliance with the law, are a mixture of individuals of different backgrounds. Companies show poor management if they ignore or tolerate a racial or ethnic slur against an employee, a supervisor, a customer or a member of the public. Such derogatory language is bad public relations for the company and causes problems between employees.

Jokes at the expense of someone else aren't jokes at all. Managers should never knowingly joke about someone's background or personal appearance or condone such behavior in their employees. One can't judge on the surface how such a joke might affect an individual. Racial or ethnic slurs stem from prejudice. Prejudice is based on stereotyped views and generalizations about a group, and shows a lack of respect for people as individuals.

Supervisors should clearly demonstrate management's attitude toward prejudice by openly showing their disapproval of any racial or ethnic slur. The supervisor may also need to interview the offender privately. The person may insist that his or her comments were harmless. The supervisor's reply should be, "Charlie, they may be *meant* to be harmless, but they have a harmful effect, so keep your thoughts to yourself."

If the problem continues, the supervisor should say, "Charlie, performance appraisals show how employees get along with the other employees and customers. I wouldn't like to place a comment on your file that you don't get along. However, if you continue to make these disparaging remarks, I'll have to place a written warning on your file. Do you understand?"

DEALING WITH PREJUDICE AGAINST WOMEN SUPERVISORS

Anti-female prejudice is found in both men and women who believe that men are superior to women and that the world should be male-dominated. This is one of the most serious problems women still face in the workplace. How should women respond to such prejudice?

Some anti-female attitudes are openly expressed, so that you're in no doubt that a particular person is out to keep women in their "place." However, many people aren't aware that their attitudes could be considered biased. These are often older men, or men whose upbringing or home situation kept women in traditionally subservient positions. Many of these men call women "dear" because women are dear to them. Such men protect women; they feel it's their duty to do so. This type of man doesn't mean to harm women and usually doesn't understand why women are offended by certain remarks. In these cases a gentle response is necessary. Use of the feedback technique will give these men the opportunity to change their behavior.

Many older women also suffer from an anti-female bias. They have been conditioned to believe women should be subservient and think of women who compete with others, supervise men or hold positions of power as unfeminine. They look down on such women, especially if they aren't married or have no intention of having children.

Anti-female attitudes are not uncommon in younger and middle-aged women. For instance, women who won't accept orders from female supervisors unconsciously feel that only men should be supervisors. They question the ability of their female supervisors and make things difficult for them.

Support staff (who are still mainly women) normally go out of their way to keep their supervisors (who are still usually male) organized, on time and comfortable. They nurture their supervisors (bring them coffee, remind them of appointments, open their mail). When a woman is appointed to a supervisory position, the nurturing may stop, unless she's on top of things. She sometimes has to let her staff know that she expects the same kind of help that the former male supervisor received.

1. Older subordinates.

Janet had a problem that at one time was rare but is quite common now. By the time she was twenty-five, she held the position of clerical supervisor. Her college education had prepared her for the position and she had four years' experience in an office. However, she found herself unprepared to supervise women almost twice her age. These women had an average of ten to fifteen years' office experience. They were openly hostile to her and quite uncooperative.

Janet decided to ask Sarah, one of the less-hostile older women, into her office to discuss the problem. Sarah was honest. She admitted she had been surprised and disappointed when Janet had been "hired off the street" as her supervisor. She had pictured someone her own age or older filling the position—possibly one of her peer group or someone whose experience she felt would give her the "right" to supervise. Instead, she found a woman the same age as her daughter in the role.

She admitted that when Janet complimented her on a job well done she felt patronized, and when she was disciplined she felt defensive. Once these feelings were brought out into the open, the two women were able to start over. Janet now understood the reasons for Sarah's antagonism and could deal with it better. Sarah had clarified why she felt as she did and made an effort to change her attitude towards Janet.

Soon Janet called a meeting with the rest of her staff to discuss the situation with them. She said that she understood how they felt and explained to them what she expected from them. She then added that she was relying on them to cooperate and asked each staff member, "Can I count on you in the future?" One employee, Julie, appeared reluctant to make such a commitment, so Janet knew she would have to keep an eye on her. Soon the woman's low productivity and negative attitude made it necessary for Janet to discipline her. She again explained to Julie what she expected from her and what the consequences would be if Julie kept on producing sloppy work. Unfortunately, Julie never did accept Janet. She kept on producing sloppy work and eventually had to be fired.

Janet fared better with the others. When she noticed a decided change in attitude and productivity, she thanked them for their understanding and cooperation.

Traditionally, society has taught us that the older woman (the mother or the aunt) knows more so therefore should be treated with respect. Switching roles is disconcerting to both the young female supervisor (who's artificially in the position of the mother) and the older female employee (who's now in the position of the daughter seeking approval). These feelings revolve around power, and who should rightly have it. There is no cut-and-dried solution to the problem.

2. Male subordinates.

Barbara supervised a staff of three men. She was an engineer and the men were technologists. Her subordinates didn't seem to listen to her and insisted on doing things their way. Fortunately, before taking the position, she had made sure that she had received proper supervisory training. This boosted her self-confidence.

Barbara found it necessary to conduct a disciplinary interview when one of her male subordinates refused to do a task assigned to him. This was a case of insubordination (a very serious infraction) that could have led to the dismissal of the employee. She handled it herself, and placed a strong written warning on the employee's file, stating that he would be fired if his negative behavior continued. She made sure her supervisor was aware of her actions, and he commended her on the competent way she had handled the touchy situation.

3. Labeling by subordinates.

Margaret, a supervisor, had been labeled "aggressive" by her subordinates and co-workers. She felt that she was just doing her job the way she had seen other supervisors do it.

She had copied her male counterparts' behavior and language. It didn't work in her case and she had been labeled an "aggressive female."

Her appearance and body language suggested that she was a forceful, self-assured, rather pushy individual. These qualities are readily accepted in men but less readily in women. I explained that her tone of voice could be the problem, or possibly her forceful body language.

Questioning revealed that she tended to give instructions in the form of orders rather than requests—"You will ..." rather than, "I would like you to ..." She agreed to tone down her speech and body language. It worked.

OTHER SUPERVISORY PROBLEMS

"My front-line people are always referring their difficult clients to me instead of handling them themselves."

Help them acquire the skills they need to deal with these difficult people (give them a copy of this book, perhaps). Explain to them how you expect them to deal with abusive, profane or threatening behavior. You may instruct them to hang up or to transfer the caller to you.

Often irate clients take all their irritability out on clerical staff and are as sweet as pie with supervisors or managers. Don't assume that your clerical staff were exaggerating about the unpleasant behavior of the client. Identify what is and is not acceptable client behavior. Support your staff when they've been mistreated. Explain to the client, "We don't tolerate harassment of our staff. I suggest you apologize to Margie about the way you spoke to her."

"Top management says we can bend the rules for special clients. My staff objects."

I don't blame them. Nothing is as annoying as saying no to clients who then go over your head, and persuade someone higher up to say yes. Support your staff by talking to your manager. Ask for some hard-and-fast rules. Explain the difficulties that have resulted. Give concrete examples, demonstrating the costs in hard feelings, poor morale, etc. The better you're prepared before you confront management, the less chance there will be that they'll turn you down. If management does turn down your request, explain what has happened to your staff.

"How can I help my staff feel comfortable when they have to enforce unpopular rules and regulations?"

Teach them the "stuck-record" technique. Request that they use this technique without raising their voices, or showing annoyance of any kind. Help them develop the necessary responses, such as, "I'm sorry. I'd like to make an exception in your case, but I can't bend the rules for anyone." Instruct them to repeat the relevant form of words as often as necessary. Be ready to back them up if someone attempts to go over their head.

"How can I handle having to cut staff, which makes four people do the work of five?"

This becomes necessary when the economy forces companies to "tighten their belts." If you haven't taken a time-management course, now's the time to do so. It will teach you how to set priorities and concentrate on the most important tasks. In doing so you will set a good example for your staff. If you help your subordinates to use good time-management techniques, you may find that four people *can* do the work of five and do so effectively.

Learn to cut corners, and try new methods for completion of tasks. Have meetings with your staff to discuss easier, quicker ways of doing tasks. Listen to their ideas carefully. Because they're the ones who are actually doing the tasks, they often come up with the best time-saving suggestions.

"My staff is always misinterpreting my instructions."

Use the paraphrasing technique to check that they have understood what you want. This technique is most effective when you're giving instructions or training someone. It will confirm to you that they "heard what you said." Be careful when asking for paraphrasing that you don't make it sound as if you think they're too dumb to understand your instructions. It is your responsibility to be sure your instructions are clear, not theirs to interpret a confusing message.

"My staff want me to spend my valuable time answering their unimportant questions."

Many supervisors may get mad at interruptions, but many others inadvertently encourage helplessness in their subordinates. When an employee comes to them with a problem, some supervisors immediately provide the solution. It would be better if they first asked, "What do you think you should do about this?" It's surprising how often the employee does know what to do. This strategy encourages independent thinking by employees. When they realize that they often have the answers already, and that you support them, they'll have more faith in their own judgment in the future.

If subordinates really don't know the answer, by all means help them. That's what you're there for.

"I hate disciplining my staff!"

It's possible that you weren't trained properly for your supervisory position. Get this training so you'll feel more comfortable when giving discipline. Remember that everything your subordinates do makes *you* look good or bad. If you allow them to do careless work, you'll be setting yourself up for a reprimand yourself. The aim of discipline is to correct poor productivity or behavior problems, not to instil a desire to retaliate in the employee. Discipline, done correctly, moves the guilt from the shoulders of the supervisor onto those of the person being disciplined. The employee is told what the consequences will be if the unacceptable behavior continues. I repeat: get supervisory training— especially in the area of employee discipline!

"I'm not quite ready to retire. How do I handle the 'heel-nippers' who want my job?"

This is tough. You don't want to move to the next level, but you shouldn't try to stop those who are young and eager from progressing. Suggest to them that they try another department and go around your position. Do everything in your power to get them ready for when you're ready to retire. If this is within two years, don't worry about the people behind you. Don't hamper them from being ready for your job or you'll just have unhappy, vindictive subordinates.

If you prove to them that you're interested not only in your own welfare, but also in theirs, they'll probably be more patient. They'll feel more comfortable if they know there will be an end to their waiting. Make it clear to them what your plans are. Explain that you're going to retire in two years. If it's longer than two years, you're probably going to spend the remainder of your employment bored to tears. If this is the case, keep working toward a more senior position yourself.

"My staff expect me to use all their bright ideas."

Judge every new idea on its own merits. Explain your conclusions, if there is some reason why it won't work. If there's some value to the idea, explain why you can or can't use the idea at that particular time. Keep encouraging your staff to come up with new ideas. After all, aren't they the ones who are actually carrying on the activities? If you stop their ideas, you'll just be demotivating them, which is the opposite of what you want.

"I have an employee who balks and wants to do things her way."

Whenever you have the ability to do so, allow your staff to complete tasks "their" way. If there's no room for flexibility in how a task is completed, be clear in your instructions. Explain that your instructions will bring about the results you want. If your employee continues to argue, ask her, "Are you refusing to do this task the way I want you do to it?" If she says, "Yes," you could rightfully charge her with insubordination. Try other methods first, but know that your only recourse may be to place a formal written warning on her file.

"My employee is very people-oriented, but is terribly disorganized. When left unsupervised he's on the phone for hours."

Use this person to make oral presentations and to deal directly with clients. Give careful, detailed instructions on what you want from him. Make sure his job description is up to date, giving standards of performance, and timelines for completion of tasks. Explain that he should not be making personal telephone calls. Initiate discipline and explain the consequences if the phone calls continue.

"My secretary is a perfectionist in everything she does, even when it's wasting valuable time. She seems to keep herself buried in her own work, doesn't seem aware of things going on around her. Because of this, she doesn't understand how her actions affect others in the department."

Give her deadlines to meet and explain the results you expect. Send her to a time-management course. If you need a draft copy of something, make sure she understands that typing errors are allowed, etc. Give her information that explains how her position fits in with others in the department. This could be by showing her a copy of the organizational chart of your section or department. Explain that when she is late with her work, it has a direct effect on others. "Margaret, when your month-end report is late, it holds up our whole department's month-end report."

"Should I be socializing with my staff?"

If you used to work with your subordinates, this may be a tough problem to solve. Remind yourself that you now have a new peer group and should be socializing with other supervisors, not your subordinates. I'm not saying you can't have coffee breaks with your staff, but don't socialize with only one or two of your staff. If you bowl with one of your subordinates, the others expect you to show favoritism to your "bowling buddy." If you *do* decide to socialize with subordinates, never discuss business! That's not fair to the other members of your staff.

conclusion

ARE YOU READY FOR SUCCESS?

You now have the tools that will enable you to deal with irate, rude, impatient, emotional, upset, persistent and aggressive people. These essential people skills will help you to handle all types of difficult individuals and situations. Learn these skills, and you can't help but improve your relationships with staff, superiors, co-workers and clients. Because these skills are now so important to businesses, this can lead to better assignments, promotions, more managerial responsibility and overall improvement in employee morale.

Your people skills will help you to control your moods and keep cool under fire. Instead of becoming defensive when dealing with an irate customer, you'll concentrate on solving the client's problem. In the end both of you will be winners.

You'll:

- be a more positive person and have more time to do what you want instead of scurrying around trying to placate others;
- be able to deal with angry or aggressive clients;
- have the skills to deal with your own anger and stress;
- be able to resist being coerced, manipulated or intimidated by the underhanded methods some people use to get their way. You'll also be able to identify and deal with the underlying problems;
- be a skillful negotiator, adept at conflict resolution;
- know how to interpret and use non-verbal signals;
- be able to identify your own and others' passive, aggressive and assertive behavior;
- know how to say no without feeling guilty;
- know how to use your communication skills to improve your effectiveness as a client, co-worker, employee or supervisor;

- know how to deal with personality clashes;
- understand the use of feedback to ensure that others are aware of how you feel about both the good and bad things they're doing;
- know how to use paraphrasing to confirm that what you heard was really what was said;
- obtain more praise and approval from your associates because you can now control your negative feelings.

Learn the techniques and practice them daily. They *do* work! Like any new skill, however, they need to be used consistently until they're automatic. When you've mastered them, you can look forward to being able to control how you deal with and react to others.

No longer will you allow others to decide what kind of day you have. Because you have gained this control, your self-esteem will rise. The more confident you are, the less stress and anxiety you'll feel and the more energy and enthusiasm you can bring to all aspects of your life. If you use these skills, you'll need to be prepared for success, because success *will* inevitably follow!

This book was written about difficult people and situations in the workplace. It has become an international bestseller, and is now available in ten languages in fourteen editions. I have also written *Dealing with Difficult Situations: At Work and at Home*, *Dealing with Difficult Spouses and Children: How to Handle Difficult Family Problems*, and *Dealing with Difficult Relatives and In-Laws*. My next publication is entitled *Workplace Bullying*.

ACKNOWLEDGEMENTS

My gratitude is extended to the thousands of participants of my seminars who contributed ideas on how they handled their difficult people.

Special thanks go to Alberta Government Telephones, who let me quote directly from several of their brochures, and my editor, Margaret Allen.

Thanks to my mother, Mabel Hastie, who taught me patience and stick-to-it-iveness, and to my daughter, Michele, who tolerated the many hours of isolation writing this book demanded of me.

BIBLIOGRAPHY

Auerback, Sylvia. "Difficult Co-workers—Handle with Care." *Computer Decisions* 13 (Dec. 1981), 178 ff.

Berne, Eric. *Games People Play.* New York: Ballantine Books, 1964.

Bernstein, Albert J., and Sydney Craft Rosen. *Dinosaur Brains.* New York: John Wiley and Sons, 1989.

Bramson, Robert M. *Coping with Difficult People.* New York: Ballantine Books, 1981.

Carnegie, Dale. *How to Win Friends and Influence People.* New York: Simon and Schuster, 1981.

Cava, Roberta. *Dealing with Difficult Situations: At Work and at Home.* Sydney: Pan Macmillan Australia, 2003.

Dealing with Difficult Spouses and Children: How to Handle Difficult Family Problems. Edmonton: Cava Management Consulting Services, 1995.

Dealing with Difficult Relatives and In-Laws. Edmonton: Cava Management Consulting Services, 2002.

Elgin, Suzette Haden. *The Last Word on the Gentle Art of Verbal Self-defense.* New York: Prentice-Hall, 1987.

Farley, Lin. *Sexual Shakedown: The Sexual Harassment of Women on the Job.* New York: McGraw-Hill, 1978.

Filley, Allan C. *Interpersonal Conflict Resolution.* Glenview, Ill.: Scott, Foresman, 1975.

Freudenberger, H.J., and G. Richelson. *Burnout.* New York: Doubleday, 1980.

Gordon, Thomas. *P.E.T.: Parent Effectiveness Training.* New York: New American Library, 1970.

Gray, John, M.D. *Men Are from Mars, Women Are from Venus: The Classic Guide to Understanding the Opposite Sex.* New York: Quill, 2004.

Hall, Edward T. *The Silent Language.* New York: Anchor Books, 1981.

Killinger, Barbara. *Workaholics: The Respectable Addicts*, revised edition. Toronto: Key Porter Books, 2004.

Levinson, Harry. *Executive Stress.* New York: New American Library, 1985.

Smith, Manuel J. *When I Say No, I Feel Guilty.* New York: Dial Press, 1975.

Tannen, Deborah. *You Just Don't Understand: Women and Men in Conversation.* New York: Quill, 2001.

Uly, William. *Getting Past No: Negotiating with Difficult People.* New York: Bantam, 1993.

Weisinger, Hendrie, and Norman M. Lobsenz. *Nobody's Perfect: How to Give Criticism and Get Results.* Los Angeles: Stradford Press, 1981.

Ziegenfuss, James T., Jr. "Responding to People Problems." *Business Horizons* 23 (Apr. 1980): 73–76.

INDEX